FOR LOVE AND MONEY

**REFLECTIONS ON THE ESSENTIAL
DISCIPLINES OF INSTITUTIONAL
INVESTMENT MANAGEMENT,
LIFE AND HAPPINESS.**

RALPH E. W. LOADER

FOR LOVE AND MONEY

Copyright ©2013 QUAERO Investment Solutions Inc
Author Ralph E. W. Loader
All rights reserved
Printed in Canada
International Standard Book Number 978-1-927355-34-3
ISBN 978-1-927355-35-0 EPUB

Published by:
Castle Quay Books
Pickering, Ontario, L1W 1A5
Tel: (416) 573-3249
E-mail: info@castlequaybooks.com   www.castlequaybooks.com

Edited by Marina Hofman Willard
Cover design by Burst Impressions

Library and Archives Canada Cataloguing in Publication

Loader, Ralph E. W., 1947-, author
    For love and money : reflections on the essential disciplines
of institutional investment management, life and happiness / Ralph E.W. Loader.

Includes bibliographical references.
ISBN 978-1-927355-34-3 (pbk.)

    1. Investments. 2. Finance, Personal. 3. Financial risk management. I. Title.

HG179.L63 2013   332.6   C2013-905366-2

CASTLE QUAY BOOKS

To Judith, the love of my life,
and with love to the generations that follow:
to Lisa and Chris, Joni and Jessie,
to Ryan and Sarah, Zachary, Zoe and Ben

ACKNOWLEDGMENTS

THIS BOOK DEALS WITH TWO SUBJECTS—INVESTMENT AND FAITH—THAT are inextricably linked. That investment and faith are intimately related may not be immediately evident to the busy and passionate securities analyst or portfolio manager. It may seem anathema to the clergyman who reads 1 Timothy 6:10, "the love of money is a root of all kinds of evil." The relationship between investment and faith, however, begins with the fact that both disciplines engage us in an endless search for truth across an ever-changing landscape. The writing of this book required a reasonable amount of research, but it springs more importantly from observation, experience and discourse. Whether you are writing a book or working out your life's plan, help is of course indispensable. But in the investment business, where the rules of competition and survival of the fittest capture most people's full attention, help is scarce. Imperfect though it may be, the faith community has rules that are quite different. For their help along the way as I shaped and continue to shape my own life's plan, and in particular the faith that drives it, I would like to thank the following people:

Don Liesemer, personal friend of many years and president of Hockey Ministries International. At the beginning of my adult search for meaning and purpose in life, Don was there. He and his family have been there ever since.

The Reverend Andrew Johnston, Minister at Briarwood Presbyterian Church, Beaconsfield, in the formative years of my Christian experience. Andrew was patient with my inexperience, called me to be an elder of the church and always challenged me. Andrew, presently the minister at St. Andrew's Church in Ottawa, has recently accepted a call to St. Andrew's Presbyterian Church in Kingston, Ontario.

The Reverend Derek Macleod, minister at Briarwood Presbyterian Church when Andrew left for Ottawa. Derek came straight out of seminary to Briarwood and is the brightest and most capable young man I have ever met. We jogged Mount Royal together while Derek shared elements of his own faith with me and explained the nature of a "calling." Judy and I also shared some time with Derek and his wife, Catherine, at a music festival in Ireland. Derek is now minister at Glenview Presbyterian Church in Toronto.

The Reverend Dr. Richard Topping, minister at The Church of St. Andrew and St. Paul, Montreal, when Judy and I moved downtown in 1999. Richard delivered consistently interesting sermons, involved me in church activities even when I was fully engaged in my career and took time to sit with me and answer my first simple questions regarding theology as they arose. He introduced me to the writings of Karl Barth. Richard is now principal of Vancouver School of Theology.

The Reverend Dr. John Vissers, principal at The Presbyterian College, Montreal, when I first met him in 2004. John taught me much about sound governance and leadership as I observed his leadership habits from a seat on the college's board of governors. In more recent years, I was able to engage John in person, through his writings and as a lecturer in my one and only postgraduate course in Christian theology, to answer questions of some complexity regarding Presbyterian Church structure and theology. John is now director of academic programs and professor of historical theology at Knox College in Toronto.

The Reverend Dr. Dale Woods, director of pastoral studies and acting principal at The Presbyterian College, Montreal. Dale has been an inspirational leader at the college and a personal mentor as I have worked to improve my understanding of the Presbyterian Church in Canada and write this book. Dale's fascination for the challenges of leadership and his interest in shaping institutional strategies to better serve humanity are exemplary.

The Reverend Jeff Veenstra, minister at The Church of St. Andrew and St. Paul, Montreal. Since 2010 Jeff has been supportive as friend, golf buddy and spiritual advisor; he has encouraged me to stay involved at various levels within our church while recognizing my service predisposition as a "sprinter," not a "marathon runner." His sensitivity in fitting me into church life where I can be most helpful without demanding long-term commitments to programs less well suited to my talents and nature has rendered my church life a real "community" experience. On the spiritual front I have observed that Jeff remains challenged by issues typical to middle-aged males who continue to worship the Toronto Maple Leafs while residing in Montreal, where hockey is religion and Les Canadiens are omnipotent.

Marina Hofman Willard, executive editor, Castle Quay Books, and PhD candidate, University of Toronto, my long-suffering editor, without whose help my search for truth in excellence would have wanted for credibility.

And I would like to thank all of the authors and contributors quoted throughout this text. I have relied heavily on the works of Daniel Migliore and Stanley Grenz, but undoubtedly all quoted works have had an important influence in shaping my personal world views, so I am indebted to the authors and originators of these works.

And finally, all credit for omissions, errors and oversights accrues entirely to this author.

CONTENTS

CHAPTER 1

Introduction—
Growing Up in Montreal

"Success is a journey not a destination.
The doing is usually more important than the outcome."
Arthur Robert Ashe Jr.

IT WAS EARLY SPRING, 1966. I WAS 18 YEARS OF AGE, AND I KNEW EXACTLY what I had to do. I was a freshman at McGill University in Montreal, a year in which I was destined to excel on the gridiron with McGill's junior varsity Indians and fail miserably in the academic arena—this in spite of my best efforts to persuade the dean of McGill's Commerce Faculty of the worthiness of my candidacy for admittance to the second year. At the time, confused and uninspired as I was about my personal future, I was able to respond with some clarity to the president of the on-campus Phi Kappa Pi fraternity when, while sharing a beer at a downtown tavern (men only in those days), he asked me, "Ralph, what do you expect to get out of your years at McGill?" The question was prescient. Moved to tears, I thought for only a moment before pronouncing, "I'm here to learn about money...about how to make it and how to hold on to it once made." I went on to share feelings of inadequacy with my mentor that evening, feelings that stemmed, I believe, from my own economically and educationally under-privileged family background. A disadvantaged economic and educational family history is very real in terms of its potential for fostering any latent sense of insecurity regarding one's knowledge of the ways of the world. But it provides as well a powerful incentive to do something about it. My mentor suggested an investment textbook, the first of many that have served to shape my philosophies of investment and of life, my character and my career of 40 years in the investment business.

This very personal exchange occurred too late in the academic year to have any significant impact on my failing grade at McGill, but it proved for me the closing chapter of those lazy, hazy, crazy teenage years in one's life, a period in which experiences and lessons learned can be so very crucial in the development of one's worldview and the shaping of one's future. Here was a turning point, a seismic shift in my personal psyche. Finally I had a goal, I had a purpose, I had a mission...and my mission was money! And thankfully, though I am not sure I understood this at the time, my purpose was much less about **making** money than it was about **understanding** money. Understanding money is, I believe, a worthy pursuit; the significance of making it is not to be underestimated, at least in part because the only credible evidence regarding one's understanding of money lies in one's experiential claims—one's proven ability to make money, lose money and come back for more.

And so I embarked, as we all do, some sooner, some later, on my life's mission. I have learned much and I have much to learn; thankfully, "success is a journey not a destination. The doing is usually more important than the outcome." But at some point, if the opportunity arises, I do think it important that we take the time necessary to reflect on the outcome of our journey to date and to commit our ideas to writing, at least for our own benefit in consolidating and understanding the rationale that supports our worldviews, certainly to open the door to others who may wish to critique our ideas and thus help us to continue learning, and at best that our ideas may be helpful to others. Forty-plus years in the business of investing and 66 years in the business of living have brought me to a point where society deems that I have earned the right to some time off—time that grants me the opportunity to put pen to paper. One really shouldn't postpone the writing for 40 years, but even at that I required a catalyst—colloquially, a "kick in the butt"—to move my ideas from space to paper. The financial crisis (now generally abbreviated as "GFC" for Global Financial Crisis) of 2008 served as that catalyst.

In terms of profound economic events we have observed much since 1970, when I first began my investment career, but the latest and most broadly significant of all of these system shocks has served as a catalyst for reflection and change across all sectors of our society. To be clear, although the financial crisis served as my inspiration to move ideas from the cerebral to the hard-drive format, the ideas themselves did not *begin* with the onset of GFC. Nor did they stem from the "dot-com bubble" (2000—2002); nor from the fallout of the various currency crises of the 1990s; nor even from the stock market's Black Monday (1987); nor from the market's numerous prior collapses in 1984, 81, 78, 74 or 70—these are all that I remember. The ideas, I believe, began taking shape when I was born, or at least in that tavern in Montreal in 1966. And they flourished in the face of youthful want—not poverty or deprivation but youthful want for a better life and for more understanding, things that were denied the generation of my parents before me. It is, as we say, "who I am." But now, in the autumn of my life, witness in my working years to all of the aforementioned remarkable economic events, shaped and moulded by these and other life experiences, finally I can affirm who I am: **I am a skeptic**. I say "finally" because with any real initiative on my own part or with conviction stemming from a greater self-confidence, I would have been able to assert my inherent nature and claim the title 30 years ago. No use pining. It is what it is; repent and move on; better late than never; **I am a skeptic, and the happier for it**.

In case you are wondering how being a skeptic (usually associated with pessimism) has anything to do with my joy-filled existence today, please permit me a brief digression; caution as to terminology is important here. Skepticism has a long history in philosophy—"philosophical skepticism"—that questions the possibility of knowledge. Philosophical skepticism has nothing to do with the title that I claim here or with any accompanying emotion. We're talking here about "methodological skepticism," which, as an approach to thought, subjects all knowledge claims to scrutiny with the goal of sorting out true from false claims. "Sorting out true from false"—there it is; more true, more happy. So I am a skeptic, sorting out true from false, finding more true and, with it, more happy. Life is beautiful. True. And even though this did not *begin* with GFC, the fallout of this particular crisis and of all of the prior significant economic events that I can recall during my working life has undoubtedly worked to influence my particular skeptical world view.

Importantly though, it is not the economic events themselves that have evoked this skepticism; rather, it is the decisions, actions and reactions of the world's best and brightest to these events that render me flabbergasted. Flabbergasted—there's a good old-fashioned word, intentionally revived here for its ability to hold your attention for at least a short while as I consider the specifics of some of the better known responses to the economic events of our time. First, though, I think it important to clarify my intent; my ideas should not be construed as criticism of those responsible for particular decisions, for hindsight has 20/20 vision and is of little help to anyone even remotely concerned with understanding the facts. Rather, my review of some of the more spectacular financial events and notable decisions in our recent past is intended as justification for my stance in favour of the skeptical worldview. Moreover, now is the time to be perfectly transparent about my objective: I am here to sell you on one idea—the idea that you and I, people of the investment world and, indeed, people in all walks of life, **need** to be more skeptical. If we are not already, together we need to become obsessed, consumed, inspired by the need to sort out true from false claims about how we should build and manage our wealth and our well-being and more importantly the wealth and the well-being of others for whom we must also accept responsibility. Anything short of this highly developed sense of skepticism and moral duty leaves us unnecessarily exposed to what King Solomon called "meaningless, a chasing after the wind" (Ecclesiastes 1:14), to what in the investment business we call "noise trader risk,"[1] a deadly investment disease deriving its meaning from Black (1986), following Kyle (1985), who identified "noise traders" as investors with no access to inside information, irrationally acting on statistical

---

[1] See J. Bradford De Long, Andrei Shleifer, Lawrence H. Summers, and Robert J. Wald-mann, "Noise Trader Risk in Financial Markets," *The Journal of Political Economy* 98 (August 1990), 703–738.

noise as if it were information that would give them an edge. Lord, spare us the anguish! Grant us truth, grant us meaning!

I have dubbed my model for a better world "GPR," the acronym for governance, policy and risk management, and the applications described herein are, to be clear, all specific to the investment world. And yet, read more broadly, the principles of GPR apply equally to all walks of life, all sectors of society. Driven by a strong and healthy skepticism, it is only by reprioritizing our efforts and energies significantly in favour of the "higher level" principles of governance, policy and risk management that we can hope to regain the upper hand on the apparent chaos fashioned by "Mr. Market." Battered and bruised as we are by Mr. Market's revered "Black Swan"[2] events, now is the time to rise up and with new disciplines take control of our own investment destinies. We are soldiers in the skeptic's war against the elements of behavioral psychology that would herd us with all other investors into the land of suboptimal decision making.

Yet there is more. As you work your way through these chapters with me, a story unfolds on three levels. On one level, lessons learned from our experiences and from the experiences of others over a tumultuous decade—1998 through 2008 and beyond—lead us to the incontrovertible conclusion that solutions lie in placing more focus on our end goals, in developing more and better controls and in giving more attention to discipline and core values, in short the principles of GPR. Call this level "resolve."

On a second level, our story is one of the failures of humanity alone to deal with these very issues. This failure is so persistent as to lead us to the inevitable questions: "What if we can't find the solutions?"; "What if we can't fix the problem?" These questions engender the skeptical mindset and raise the question "How do we respond to failure?" Call this second level "humility."

Our final chapters deal with this eventuality, and we expand our model for a better world accordingly to a third level with a word on

---

[2] This term was popularized by Nassim Nicholas Taleb, *The Black Swan: The Impact of the Highly Improbable* (New York: Random House, 2007, 2010), and is defined as an event, positive or negative, that is deemed improbable yet causes massive consequences.

faith. So this is *My Little Book on Investment Governance, Policy, Risk Management and Faith* (GPRF) in which we advocate neither arrogance nor fear nor capitulation in the face of human weakness. We advocate instead careful planning, organization, implementation and controls to address our weaknesses, coupled with an ever-present skepticism, **first of ourselves**, together yielding a clear conviction that with resolve, with humility and with faith we can build a better, fairer, more certain world in which to invest our money and our lives.

The idea that faith holds out promise for a better investment world is, some would say, controversial. Others would label the idea a contradiction in terms. How does faith work in a world of investing that we characterize symbolically by the emotions of greed (the bull) and fear (the bear)? Is it too much of a stretch to contemplate useful metaphors between spirituality and money? Between truth and investing other people's money? Between faith and Wall Street?

In my 62nd year of growing up in Montreal and early into my first year of experimentation with the concepts and possibilities attendant to a retired or semi-retired lifestyle, I considered this question and decided it was a worthy one—worthy at least of some thought, some research and some effort to record my conclusions. Admittedly my first days of this undertaking were cloaked in mystery and wonder. I began with an intuitive sense that a sound spiritual grounding would somehow prove beneficial to one's investment acumen; I even felt that somewhere during my career, or perhaps throughout it, I had experienced the effect first-hand. But I was unable to conjure up a clear picture of the model, of the flowchart linking spirituality through investment beliefs to investment strategy, or much about its beneficial nature. By my count the word "money" is used more than 30 times in the first four books (Matthew, Mark, Luke and John) of the New Testament alone, many times by Jesus. I am sure that fact had some bearing on my intuition. But intuition, the most basic of human emotions, is a beautiful and simultaneously very inhibiting thing—you have this feeling that something is true but you can't explain why it is so. Your rational mind will not permit you to act on intuitive intelligence because you have no visible or scientifically provable reason to support your action. Handcuffed!

But two years into my research the fog began to lift, and two years further on dusk gave way to dawn and dawn to a shiny new day. There really is a relationship between money and spirituality, and I have lived it—not from the first day of my investment career, but thankfully more so with the passage of time and a few hard-won lessons. Faith, I have learned, is fundamental to my ability to live out my investment beliefs. It is much more than intuition; it is the enabling confidence that permits me to act on sound investment information and to ignore statistical noise. It is the humility that keeps me working into the night, ever skeptical of my own decision-making ability. It is the knowledge that empowers me to understand that information relating to an investment firm's philosophy, process and historical performance is useful for generating questions, not for providing answers. And it is the judgment necessary to discern between investment professionals who place their clients' interests ahead of their own and those whose motivations are less trustworthy. These beliefs are at the core of a much broader set of investment beliefs that I have built over 40-plus years in the business, but it is my faith that informs these beliefs and that enables me to act on them. Chapter 2 begins the story that proved the catalyst for my convictions.

Can faith move us from this…

The Bull and Bear Statues at the Frankfurt Stock Exchange in Frankfurt, Germany.
The Frankfurt Stock Exchange is the world's 12th largest exchange by market capitalization.

…to this?

The Wall Street Bull sculpture, also called the Charging Bull or the Bowling Green Bull, is one of the symbols of the financial district in Manhattan. The famous 7,000 pound bronze statue was created by Arturo Di Modica and installed near Wall Street to "bring bulls back to Wall Street" after the 1987 stock market crash. This picture is digitally modified with the insertion of the bear to depict a harmonious rather than adversarial relationship between bull and bear.

Like this familiar image of Wall Street anchored by Trinity Church, is there justification for anchoring our investment beliefs in the spiritual foundations of our faith?

Trinity Church at 79 Broadway, Lower Manhattan, is a historic, active, well-endowed parish church in the Episcopal Diocese of New York. Trinity Church is at the intersection of Wall Street and Broadway in New York.

CHAPTER 2

The Global Financial Crisis—
We're Not as Smart as We Think We Are!

"The secret, the best-kept secret is
That the most famous painter in the world, which I am,
Does not yet know how to go about painting."
Salvador Dali

Since 1998, two economic events in particular have worked to consolidate my thinking and that, I am sure, of many other like-minded investment skeptics. Both events elicited my shock, and indeed the world's shock, at the realization that the complexity of issues encountered within the realm of finance and economics is such that those empowered publically or through private enterprise to render decisions bear a high risk of failure. Even the best and the brightest of our leaders in the public or private sectors of the financial community, with the power to impact the world's financial stability, are uncertain in many instances of the broader implications of their decisions. These events are just two of the many repeated instances over the past two decades that served to heighten our awareness of humanity's ineptness at dealing with the complex structures that we have built for ourselves and within which we work on a daily basis.

The first of these events was the collapse of Long-Term Capital Management (LTCM), a hedge fund management firm based in Greenwich, Connecticut. The firm was founded by John Meriwether, formerly of Salomon Brothers. He was joined by several brilliant men, heroes in the world of academic finance and heroes of mine through my years of undergraduate and postgraduate study in finance and well into the advanced years of my career in the investment business. These men included Robert Merton and Myron Scholes, who received the Nobel Prize in economics in 1997. Like so many asset management teams that I have researched over the span of my career, the LTCM team showed remarkable prescience in its formative years, only to come unravelled as their success was discovered by big money seeking big returns. In my experience, many such firms fail simply because their singular investment style that is favoured by the market for a period of time suddenly goes out of favour and stays that way long enough that initially enamoured investors lose patience. In the case of LTCM, however, the founders' greatest strength also proved their Achilles heel and compounded the effect of their collapse by virtue of its extended impact on other institutions. The founders were brilliant mathematicians and understood well the intricacies of options pricing and the potential of leverage. Unfortunately, weak market conditions in 1998 were followed by the Russian currency crisis and credit events in many emerging markets that worked against the market exposures assumed by LTCM. Finally, "in September 1998 the Federal Reserve organized a rescue of long-term capital management because it was concerned about the possibility of dire consequences for world financial markets if it allowed the firm to fail."[3]

Since then we have wondered at the reality that 16 of the world's foremost academics and practitioners together failed so spectacularly. Warren Buffett has said that these people were not only brilliant and experienced but also good people who had their own money invested alongside that of their clients. Yet he notes that with all of that intellectual power and sound governance practices, "to make money that they didn't have and didn't need, they risked what they did have and did need... and that's foolish; that is just plain foolish." Facetiously, and with an endearing measure of humility, Buffet adds, "If I ever write a book it will

---

[3] Kevin Dowd, "Too Big to Fail? Long-Term Capital Management and the Federal Reserve," *Cato Institute Briefing Papers* 52 (September 1999), 2.

be called, *Why Smart People Do Dumb Things.* My partner says it should be autobiographical!"[4]

If the LTCM event didn't get your attention, my second "aha moment" certainly did. Ten years later, the Global Financial Crisis, signalled by the undoing of the U.S. sub-prime mortgage market and the resulting collapse of related derivative instruments, and marked notably by the failure of Bear Stearns (Bear), proved beyond any reasonable doubt my thesis regarding humanity's intellectual fragility. How could so few, serving their own interests, have successfully managed to manipulate a carefully developed and monitored financial system to impoverish so many over such a short period of time? The following timeline of selected events leading up to and following on from the crash paints a clear picture of the foolishness that we exhibit so consistently when dealing with other people's money, and even when dealing with our own.

Origins: The New Millennium (2002 to 2006)

Much of the debate around the GFC has focused on discerning the causes of the crisis and who can be blamed. In this work, I make no attempt to lay blame or to pinpoint specific causes. Rather, I seek to understand what is in the nature of humanity that contributed most to our undoing and to discover how we can manage our nature toward better outcomes. Investment professionals and pundits will be intimately familiar with the origins and essence of the sub-prime crisis. For the more casual reader, I offer the following analysis of the sub-prime crisis, an extract from the Knowledge@Wharton website, where much more is available to those interested in information, ideas and opinions on the sub-prime crisis, an important catalyst and arguably a major cause of the GFC.

The crisis had its roots in the U.S. housing boom that began early in the decade. In previous decades, most mortgages were backed by the Federal Housing Administration and government-authorized companies Fannie Mae and Freddie Mac, which bought mortgages and bundled them into high-grade securities that were then sold to investors in the

---

4 Warren Buffet, Buffett Lecture at the University of Florida School of Business, October 15, 1998.

form of bonds. Investors shared rights to homeowners' principal and interest payments.

But from 2002 through 2006 the market changed, says Wharton real estate professor Susan M. Wachter. A growing portion of mortgages were issued by firms not backed by Fannie, Freddie and the FHA—and not bound by the same legal requirements to deal only in investment-grade loans and securities. Wall Street had taken over the role of packaging the mortgages into marketable securities and Wall Street alchemists found new ways to turn risky mortgages—subprime loans originally designed for borrowers with low income or poor credit—into securities that looked almost risk-free. Investors were eager to buy these securities, which promised higher yields than U.S. Treasury bonds and other "safe" holdings.

Underwriting standards hit bottom in 2006, Wachter says. Many lenders required no down payment at all, no longer demanded proof of an applicant's income and offered very low teaser rates. Some "option" loans allowed borrowers to essentially pay whatever they wanted to each month, with shortages added to the principal, or remaining debt. This process, called 'negative amortization,' can leave the borrower owing more and more as time goes by. In a standard mortgage, the debt gradually shrinks.

Although the growing risks were clear to people who understood the mortgage and housing markets, lenders kept lending because they could earn big up-front fees. They were not terribly concerned if homeowners defaulted later, Wachter says, because the loans were converted into securities that passed the risks on to investors.

But cracks began to appear in 2006. Most subprime loans carried adjustable interest rates, and growing numbers of borrowers were falling behind after annual interest-rate resets pushed up their monthly payments. By the summer of 2007, prices of securities based on subprime loans were in free fall, as investors worried they would not get the interest and principal payments promised. Surprised about the depth of this problem, investors started to lose confidence in many other types of securities based on various forms of debt. Lenders became reluctant to lend.[5]

---

[5] Taken from "Subprime Crisis: A Bouquet of Opportunity Masked a Reek of Risk," *Knowledge@Wharton* (June 20, 2008) and "Subprime Crisis: Could New Rules Avert Another Credit Crisis? Perhaps, but Be Wary," *Knowledge@Wharton* (June 20, 2008).

Spread of the Crisis (2007 through 2008[6])

Early in 2007 defaults on subprime loans escalated and we watched with some trepidation as subprime lending firms, one after another including New Century, the largest player in the business, declared bankruptcy. It followed that the asset-backed securities that were created from these failing sub-prime loans would also experience losses, and it was not long before Bear Stearns suffered significant losses in hedge funds that it had built on the back of its own initiatives in the asset-backed securities business.

As the first of the failures of so many financial institutions, the Bear story provides a template of initial behavior and response that was witnessed again and again from 2007 through 2009 as the necessary process called "deleveraging" unfolded. The following summarizes elements of the Bear story that are relevant to this book's central point. Our source is CNNMoney, where William Cohan excerpts his own book *House of Cards: A Tale of Hubris and Wretched Excess on Wall Street*. It is the *human* element that interests me here. Cohan uses the word "hubris," and if you have to choose a single word I suppose hubris is as good as any. But the varied forms of negative behavioural response to the pressures inherent in the investment business are the stuff of legend. Greed, fear, jealousy, poor judgment, foolishness, wilful blindness, dishonesty, and corruption are just a few of the other words we might apply. Of course, ego is at the centre of the behaviour described by all of these terms, and the wonder of ego is its potential to be our friend or our enemy. Former Bear CEO Alan Schwartz assigns responsibility collectively to a broad group of institutions, but the story as set out in the following Cohan excerpts highlights the importance of individual behaviour, i.e., leadership or the lack thereof, to the ultimate outcome. Here's the story:

> Bear Stearns, the fifth-largest U.S. investment bank, survived the 9/11 attacks unscathed, just as it had survived unscathed every other major crisis since its founding in 1923, among them: the

---

[6] Unless otherwise footnoted, this section is extracted from "The Great Contraction: Timeline of Events," Economics of Crisis. Available at http://www.economicsofcrisis.com/economics_of_crisis/timeline.html.

Great Depression, World War II and the 1987 market crash. Indeed, until the very end, the firm had never had a losing quarter in its history. But in the months following 9–11, James Cayne and his senior management team, including Alan "Ace" Greenberg, Warren Spector and Alan Schwartz would unwittingly sow the seeds of the firm's destruction by betting heavily on the manufacture and the sale of mortgage-backed securities.

In the short run, the decision by Bear's executives to become a leader in this business resulted in huge profits for the firm— and massive paychecks for them. Along with bankers at Lehman Brothers, Merrill Lynch and Morgan Stanley, they were only too happy to capitalize on the mortgage boom that occurred in the wake of 9–11 when the Federal Reserve loosened the money supply.

One of Bear Stearns profit centers was a small hedge-fund division. The firm seeded it with a relatively trifling $45 million equity investment. Ralph Cioffi (pronounced Chee-off-ee), a long-time Bear Stearns fixed income salesman turned hedge fund manager, ran it. The funds were part of the firm's relatively tiny asset management business, known as BSAM. BSAM reported to Warren Spector, Bear's resident wunderkind, who as the firm's co-president (with Alan Schwartz) was responsible for overseeing 90% of its revenue, including its massive fixed-income business.

Like Cayne and Ace Greenberg, the boyish Spector was a world-class bridge player and many people both inside and outside Bear Stearns considered it inevitable that he would one day soon run the firm. In October 2003, Spector's friend Cioffi moved from Bear's fixed income department to BSAM and set up a hedge fund, called the High-Grade Structured Credit Fund, with money from outside investors. The fund eventually would have around $1.5 billion of investors' cash in it. Then 47, Cioffi had joined Bear Stearns in 1985 as an institutional fixed income salesman, specializing in structured finance products.

Cioffi grew up in South Burlington, Vermont, near Lake Champlain. From 1989 to 1991, he was the New York head of fixed income sales and then, for the next three years, served as global product and sales manager for high-grade credit products. As a salesman, Cioffi covered the Ohio Public Employees Retirement System account and was making around $4 million, year after year. "He was the top fixed income salesman in a firm where fixed income was king," said one senior managing director.

"We all grew up with Ralph here," explained Paul Friedman, who was the chief operating officer of Bear's fixed-income division. "Ralph is one of the smartest guys I've ever met and was absolutely the best salesman I've ever met. When I was a trader, he was a salesman, a fabulous salesman. He was incredibly personable, incredibly smart, creative and could get things done." As a manager, Cioffi was another story. "He had adult ADD," says Friedman…not long after July 30, 2007 Cioffi and Tannin were fired. On August 1 Jimmy Cayne fired Warren Spector. On January 2008, Cayne resigned as CEO, probably within days of a coup d'état that was percolating throughout the firm's corridors. (Cayne remained the Chairman of the firm's board of directors.)

Ralph Cioffi is escorted by police officers out of 26 Federal Plaza in New York, U.S., on June 19, 2008. Mr. Cioffi was acquitted of all charges in November 2009, but according to a Bloomberg news report on February 13, 2012, he agreed to pay $800,000 and accept a three-year ban from the securities industry to settle a related civil case brought by the U.S. Securities and Exchange Commission.

With both Cayne and Spector dispatched, Bear Stearns had little choice but to turn to Alan Schwartz, the firm's most prominent investment banker, and ask him to be the CEO, the first time an investment banker had run the firm, which had always been predominantly a fixed income shop. As respected as Schwartz was on Wall Street, he had little knowledge of the world of trading and fixed income, let alone the billions of dollars of complex, mortgage-related securities that were larding the firm's balance sheet. He decided not to raise additional equity capital for the firm or to seek a merger partner. He determined Bear Stearns could continue to go it alone and succeed.

That was yet another fateful decision. Within two months of his appointment as CEO, investors, repo lenders, hedge-fund clients and trading counterparties all began to question the firm's efficacy—the endgame that began nine months earlier with the disaster in Cioffi's hedge funds. The failure of Bear Stearns during the four days beginning March 12, 2008, culminating in its sale for a pittance to JPMorgan Chase on March 16, meant that no firm on Wall Street could any longer be considered safe, especially those firms such as Lehman Brothers, Merrill Lynch and Citigroup that had even more mortgage-related securities on their balance sheets than did Bear Stearns. The historic unwind of 2008 had begun…Former Bear CEO Alan Schwartz has told friends that he sees their role this way, "These things happen and they're big, and when they happen everybody tries to look at what happened in the previous six months to find someone or something to blame it on. But, in truth, it was a team effort. We all f***ed up. Government. Rating agencies. Wall Street. Commercial banks. Regulators. Investors. Everybody."[7]

The Bear Stearns story gives us a sense of the psychological drama that unfolded and then exploded on company premises and that reverberated throughout the world's financial community. Cohan's narrative also

---

[7] William Cohan, "Inside the Bear Stearns Boiler Room," *CNNMoney* (March 4, 2009) and William Cohan, "Where are they now?" *CNNMoney* (March 4, 2009).

affords us insight into the cultural dynamics of the organization—not just of Bear, but on a much broader scale, always respectful of exceptions, of the financial sector in general and of firms, families and working groups of people in any environment when placed under stress. Alan Schwartz's concluding remarks wherein he allocates blame broadly to a "team effort" are particularly revealing. Senior executives at the firm (in government, at rating agencies, on Wall Street and in regulatory bodies) are roundly criticized by the media and the bureaucracy; they resign, they are fired, they are arrested and charged with the most serious of white-collar crimes. But from a secular world perspective, these are not stupid people. Indeed, they are extremely bright people, dynamic leaders, the best and the brightest that we have. Yet they "f***ed up"! To the point I made in the introduction regarding this Bear Stearns saga, it is the human element that interests me here; indeed the human element—hubris, wretched excess and folly—inherent in human decision making. If we can't trust the judgment of our best and brightest, what does that say for the ability of the rest of us to manage the complex institutional structures that we have built over the past century or two? What does that say for the ability of the rest of us to understand the relationships between complex financial instruments, to forecast outcomes or to manage risk even at micro-economic levels? It says, "We can't." And if we can't, should we not "confront the brutal facts,"[8] confront them with renewed skepticism, with heightened determination to sort out true from false claims regarding responsible governance, investment policies and ideas about how to manage risk?

If the conclusions that I draw from the LTCM and Bear stories have not yet convinced you that **you** have a role to play in the making of a better investment world, then consider the implications of the following—just some of the better known events at the better known firms in the domino effect post the announcement of Bear Stearns' hedge fund losses. If you are in the investment business and have a good knowledge of these events, you may wish to skip this section and go directly to my conclusions in the last paragraph of this chapter 2. For

---

[8] Phraseology from Jim Collins, *Good to Great: Why Some Companies Make the Leap... and Others Don't* (New York: HarperCollins Publishers, 2001).

those not in the business or for those not convinced of the conclusions that I draw from the observations at LTCM and at Bear, the section serves to reinforce by repetition examples of the same human behaviour (what Salvador Dali humbly refers to as his own "buffoonery") witnessed at LTCM and at Bear and the consequences thereof.

The Narrative Unfolds (2007 through 2008 continued)

Later, in 2007, the extent of popularity of the asset (mortgage)-backed invention became more apparent as hedge funds and banks, small and large, began to reveal their exposures to these securities. Liquidity in these securities dried up as prices plummeted and banks in particular faced immediate problems with their declared regulatory capital positions. In September, Northern Rock received emergency funding from the Bank of England, and depositors lined up to withdraw their monies, adding fuel to the fire as withdrawals served to worsen the bank's capital position.

As the year drew to a close, E. Stanley O'Neal vacated the post of president, chief executive officer and chairman of the board of Merrill Lynch in the wake of multi-billion dollar losses and write-downs; he was succeeded by John Thain.[9]

With US government encouragement, JPMorgan Chase bought Bear Stearns in March 2008 for a price of $10 per share, compared to trading prices of $170 per share one year earlier. Later in the year, the US government moved to take control of Fannie Mae (the Federal National Mortgage Association) and Freddie Mac (the Federal Home Loan Mortgage Corporation), America's two largest mortgage companies. The significance of this move is historic in proportion as Fannie Mae was first created in 1938 to ease the impact of the Great Depression on mortgage lenders and to afford otherwise non-creditworthy borrowers a source of capital for housing purposes. Freddie Mac was created in 1970 with a similar mandate, and both companies ultimately became publicly traded entities.

---

[9] Jenny Anderson and Landon Thomas Jr., "NYSE Chief Is Chosen to Lead Merrill Lynch," *The New York Times* (November 14 2007).

In September 2008, Bank of America bought Merrill Lynch, and on September 15, *The Wall Street Journal* reported, "the (all-stock) deal values Merrill at $29 a share."[10] *Forbes* added,

> Chief Executive Officer John Thain arguably won Merrill's shareholders fair compensation, given that Bank of America's offer represents a 70.1% premium from Friday's closing price. Nonetheless, Bank of America is acquiring the 94-year-old firm at a 61% discount from its year-ago price, when it was trading at roughly $75 a share.[11]

In the same month, Lehman Brothers filed for bankruptcy protection. The US government's decision not to step in remains hotly debated, as Lehman's failure resulted in a domino effect, creating major stresses and failures throughout the financial and real estate markets. Barclays PLC stepped in to buy selected divisions of Lehman, and through it all,

> as the credit crisis worsened, Lehman's Richard S. Fuld Jr. was Wall Street's one seemingly Teflon chief executive, keeping his job unchallenged even as CEOs fell at rivals like Bear, Merrill Lynch Cos Inc. and Citigroup and as Fuld's own underlings, including Chief Financial Officer Erin Callan, were pushed out.[12]

And then there was AIG, yet another US government bailout in September 2008. AIG was an interesting study because, as an insurance company, it was on the other side of many of the mortgage-backed deals that investors held. The more savvy investors in mortgage-backed securities tended to hedge their bets by purchasing mortgage default insurance on some of their holdings. Insurance premiums reduced the

---

[10] Matthew Karnitschnig, Carrick Mollenkamp, and Dan Fitzpatrick, "Bank of America to Buy Merrill," *The Wall Street Journal* (September 15, 2008).

[11] Evelyn Rusli, "The Universal Appeal of Bank of America," *Forbes* (November 15, 2008).

[12] Christian Plumb and Dan Wilchins, "Lehman CEO Fuld's Hubris Contributed to Meltdown," *Reuters* (September 14, 2008).

investor's income stream but protected them against the default, which turned out to be the greater of the risks. AIG, who sold the default insurance on these vehicles, was left holding the bag. "The company lost $13.2 billion in the first six months of 2008, largely owing to declining values in mortgage-related securities held in its investment portfolio and collateralized debt obligations it owned."[13] AIG replaced Martin Sullivan as its chief executive and named Robert B. Willumstad, formerly of Citigroup, as its new leader. On September 22, 2008, AIG was removed from the Dow Jones Industrial Average.

As liquidity pressures mounted everywhere through the remainder of 2008, even Goldman Sachs and Morgan Stanley converted to bank holding companies so that they could access federal reserve bank lending. In the UK the British government assumed control of mortgage lender Bradford and Bingley while Europe saw government capital injections into Fortis, the Belgian banking and insurance company, and Hypo Real Estate, a large commercial property lender in Germany.

Finally, the year concluded with a government rescue mission for Citigroup. *The New York Times* reported, "the complex rescue plan calls for the government to back about $306 billion in loans and securities and directly invest about $20 billion in Citigroup."[14] A year earlier, Charles Prince had resigned from his post as chairman and CEO of Citigroup following a reported 57 percent drop in quarterly profits and write-downs resulting from losses in the sub-prime mortgage market. He was replaced as chairman by former US treasury secretary Robert Rubin, while Sir Win Bischoff served as interim chief executive.[15] In 2008, *Fortune* named Charles Prince as one of eight economic leaders "who didn't [see] the crisis coming," noting his overly optimistic statements in July 2007.

---

[13] Michael de la Merced and Gretchen Morgensen, "A.I.G. Allowed to Borrow Money From Subsidiaries," *The New York Times* (September 14, 2008).

[14] Eric Dash, "Citigroup to Halt Dividend and Curb Pay," *The New York Times* (November 23, 2008).

[15] "Citigroup chief executive resigns," *BBC News* (November 5, 2007). See also Landon Thomas Jr. and Eric Dash, "Shake-up at Citigroup," *The New York Times* (October 12, 2007).

As the subprime storm was brewing, Prince famously scoffed at the idea it could hurt his bank. Citing Citi's then-plentiful liquidity, he told the *Financial Times* in July 2007: "...as long as the music is playing, you've got to get up and dance. We're still dancing."[16]

Robert Rubin expressed his own regrets that he too, from his senior position at Citigroup, failed to foresee the financial crisis:

> Almost all of us involved in the financial system, including financial firms, regulators, ratings agencies, analysts and commentators missed the powerful combination of forces at work and the serious possibility of a massive crisis...We all bear responsibility for not recognizing this, and I deeply regret that.[17]

The Citigroup story is one more very good example of our ineptness at dealing with the complex structures that we have built for ourselves and within which we work on a daily basis. You need only google Charles Prince or Robert Rubin and review their experiential and academic backgrounds to understand that the knowledge and influence that these men wield is impressive; yet they and so many other equally talented institutional leaders failed all of us, working within the global financial system that we all thought they knew best.

Have you been counting? The casualties mounted through 2008 and well into 2009. When measured in dollars or failed institutions, the numbers are staggering. But dollars and failed institutions are not the issue—they're just the symptoms, as it were, of a much greater problem. The problem we are concerned with is **people**. Yes, people's careers and people's lives, but above all, we're concerned with people's virtually unlimited capacity for rationalization in the name of dollars and institutions. We're concerned with just how consistently our capacity for rationalization leads to decisions that compromise our intelligence

---

[16] Katie Benner and Christopher Tkaczyk, "8 Who Saw the Crisis Coming...and 8 Who Didn't," *CNNMoney* (August 2008).

[17] Eamon Javers, "Robert Rubin Returns," *Politico* (April 8, 2010).

(misleading ourselves) and, in the worst cases, compromise our integrity (misleading others). A few of the higher profile people casualties since Bear Stearns were previously noted: E. Stanley O'Neal, Merrill Lynch; Richard S. Fuld Jr., Lehman Brothers; Joseph Cassano, AIG; Charles O. "Chuck" Prince and Robert Rubin, Citigroup. Are all of these people so incompetent, so dull, as to lead their companies and their countries, not to mention their families and their own personal lives, to the brink of disaster? I think not. I am reminded of Warren Buffett's book-in-the-making, *Why Smart People Do Dumb Things*. The answer is, I think, "We're Not as Smart as We Think We Are!" And so we have every right—in fact we have every responsibility—to be skeptical…yes, of others, *but first and most importantly of ourselves.*

In our next chapter, we take a critical look at the culture that we have spawned in the investment industry over decades of occasionally stable but mostly changing and volatile economic environments. We consider why the industry as we know it needs to embrace change—deep cultural change—if we are to survive the new age of technology and all it implies for the accessibility of information and the need for transparency.

CHAPTER 3

The Need for Change— Culture Gone Awry

"Culture: the cry of men in face of their destiny."
Albert Camus

"Every aspect of Western culture needs a new code of ethics—a rational ethics—as a precondition of rebirth."
Ayn Rand

IN HIS NUMBER ONE BESTSELLER *LIAR'S POKER*, MICHAEL LEWIS TELLS stories that brilliantly portray a corporate culture that is prevalent at very many—let me hasten to say, not all—global investment brokerage firms. In praise of *Liar's Poker*, Tom Wolfe, author of *Bonfire of the Vanities*, says "*Liar's Poker* is the funniest book on Wall Street I've ever read." Funny, but "funny" wasn't the first word that came to mind when I read the book. The book does capture a certain locker-room humour that is sadly typical of investment dealer trading desks, but better descriptors were phrases like "right on the mark" (*People* magazine), "wonderfully insightful" (*New York* magazine) and "one of those rare works that encapsulate and define an era" (*Fortune* magazine). *Newsweek* called the book "a wry, wicked account." Personally, I would label the stark reality that this book conveys "scary," and I think we should emphasize that the "era" encapsulated is still unfolding. The beat goes on; arrogance at senior levels, a sense of entitlement at more junior levels, free-wheeling

RALPH E. W. LOADER

sarcasm and unconstrained disrespect for one's colleagues creates a "me first" culture where the client's interests inevitably get lost in the shuffle. In my personal experience, bond desks (contrasted to stock trading desks) typically create a subculture of their own, setting the standard for coarse behavior. Exemplifying that behavior is the story of Jeffery Kronthal, a trainee at Salomon Brothers in the "Class of 1979."

> [Kronthal] was a junior clerk under Peter Marro...his primary responsibility was to keep track of the bond position run by John D'Antona.
>
> Kronthal had just graduated from the five-year Wharton combined undergraduate and MBA program...and he had more elevated interests than Johnny's positions. This displeased Johnny. Johnny would lean back in his chair and ask, "Jeffery, what's the position?"
>
> Jeffery would say, "I don't know."
>
> Johnny would scream at Lewie, "What the f***'s going on? The clerk doesn't know the positions."
>
> Lewie would scream at Peter, "What the f*** is going on? Your clerk doesn't know the positions."
>
> Peter would scream at Jeffery, "Why don't you know the positions?"
>
> And Jeffery would shrug.[18]

Setting aside what this exchange may imply about risk management practices in the industry, it is a fact that profanity of this sort is standard fare on many trading desks and betrays something of the standards of behavior that are set by corporate leadership at many of the world's leading brokerage firms. And what do these standards spawn in respect of fiduciary accountability for the client's assets? Consider the implications of the following story for standards of honesty and integrity within a company or an industry:

---

[18] Michael Lewis, *Liar's Poker: Rising Through the Wreckage on Wall Street* (New York: Penguin Books, 1990), 95.

Through a loudspeaker, known as the hoot and holler, a man on 41 [the 41st floor] hooted and hollered at the salesmen on 40 to sell more bonds. I once walked through when the firm was attempting to sell the bonds of the drugstore chain Revco (which later went bankrupt and defaulted on those very bonds). The voice boomed out of the box: "C'mon, people, we're not selling truth!" Life on the 40th was grim.[19]

Obviously there was no room for the skeptic on the 40th floor at Salomon Brothers, no room for sorting out true from false claims in the client's interests. This culture—firm first, client second—prevails today throughout the industry, and the industry's opacity to anyone on the outside is such that no casual observer, no occasional regulatory inspection, can unearth either its existence or its impact on client wealth.

Lewis's take on investment industry culture is made current in his book *The Big Short*.[20] A shorter and fascinating read with stories of several industry participants who anticipated the unfolding of the crisis (notably Steve Eisman of FrontPoint Partners, a subsidiary of Morgan Stanley) may be found in Lewis' article "The End,"[21] which characterizes the new post-crisis era as the end of Wall Street as we knew it. In his article, Lewis quotes Vincent Daniel, Steve Eisman's colleague, who shares with us some of Eisman's wisdom in relation to sub-prime lenders: "The one thing Steve always says," Daniel explains, "is you must assume they are lying to you. They will always lie to you." This references an industry culture that I fear has not seen the end. Market aficionados, though, will appreciate the picture that formed part of the article:

---

[19] Lewis, *Liar's Poker*, 62.

[20] Michael Lewis, *The Big Short* (New York: W. W. Norton & Company, 2010). In this book, Lewis captures the technical elements underpinning the financial crisis and reveals more about the essence of investment industry culture that drove so many failed decisions through the worst days of the GFC.

[21] Michael Lewis, "The End," *Portfolio* (November 11, 2008).

THE END, by Michael Lewis Nov 11 2008
Photo illustration by Ji Lee

For the investor, institutional or retail, the moral of the story is simple: *Caveat emptor*—hail the skeptic!

But what can the industry do of its own accord to mend its ways, to become a force for positive change in the investment world and beyond? Judging by the state of the bull pictured here, nothing short of a revival (perhaps a resurrection!) will suffice. Certainly we need change, and that's never easy, so in the next chapter I have worked to uncover two dynamic change agents that I believe are mandatory to the design and assembly of the operating framework that is required to modify behavior, build more enduring cultures and enable more effective investment decision making.

CHAPTER 4

The Agents of Change—
Leadership and Core Values

"The only ones among you who will be really happy are those who have sought and found how to serve."
Albert Schweitzer

SKEPTICISM SETS THE COURSE FOR A BETTER INVESTMENT WORLD; but alas, skepticism is not enough. It is one of those "necessary but insufficient" conditions for better investment decisions. Highly skeptical people contribute to effective risk control by raising our awareness of the potential pitfalls inherent in particular courses of action. They help by protecting us from ill-considered action, but they are much less effective at prioritizing the needs of an organization and identifying the best course of action for the achievement of those needs. Skepticism is a beginning, but the fruits of skepticism alone are *indecision* and *inaction*. Skepticism must therefore be augmented by a framework for actionable decisions as we move from my central philosophical stance—to be skeptical, seek the truth and keep working at it 'til you die—towards the more practical essentials of a model for smarter investing (the model, you will recall, that I have dubbed "GPR"). To this point we have engaged primarily in "big-picture" philosophical thinking, and as with much philosophical thought, our discussion has surfaced more questions than answers. In this and subsequent chapters, as we search for answers to our questions, we reach deep into the *culture* of an organization in ways that are essential to effect meaningful and positive change. And by now it must be clear that the business of investment management, investment brokerage and investment banking is a business seriously in need of meaningful and positive change.

If skepticism is our formational philosophy, where do we look to build on that foundation towards the creation of an essential framework for actionable decisions?

For several months in the aftermath of the market collapse in September 2008, I kept a journal of the writings of some of my favourite market watchers. In every instance, the facts and arguments asserted by these authors confirm that the people of the investment industry, even the best and brightest of them, possess little truth and less understanding; hail the skeptic! Several of these writers give us glimpses of the thinking that I believe we need to embrace to create a meaningful framework for actionable decisions. Our framework and our thinking, I propose, must rest on a foundation of strong leadership and core values. As you read through the following journal entries, consider whether these foundational themes speak to you as they did to me.

Friday, October 24, 2008:
Alan Greenspan Reflects on our Hubris and on our Limitations

In an article from today's *Globe and Mail*, Alan Greenspan sheds some light on his own perspectives during his tenure as the Federal Reserve chairman. I find a couple of his statements particularly relevant to the points I am making here, and I offer comment on both. First, he says,

> I made a mistake in presuming that the self-interests of organizations, specifically banks and others, were such that they were best capable of protecting their own shareholders and their equity in the firms…Something which looked to be a very solid edifice and, indeed, a critical pillar to market competition and free markets did break down. And I think that…shocked me. I still do not fully understand why it happened.[22]

---

[22] Barrie McKenna, "Greenspan admits 'mistake' on bank regulation," *Globe and Mail* (October 24, 2008).

I think I understand why it happened. The breakdown is a function of poor governance (the "G" in my GPR Model), in particular the misalignment of time horizons—those of corporate management and those of most other shareholders. Most shareholders are long-term investors—15, 20 or 50 years. Management is concerned with the term of their employment contract, or worse yet, with the term over which they can potentially build their personal financial security—3 to 5 years, shorter if possible. Management therefore can readily appear to be working towards share price maximization in the short run while engaging in transactions that put the longer term viability of an enterprise in serious jeopardy. As we contemplate the measures of success for almost any venture, we tend to give too little consideration to the appropriate time horizon over which our selected measures should be applied. It's all about governance and, in this case, particularly about the time horizons over which compensation packages are structured. But importantly, Dr. Greenspan, and in fairness most of the rest of us, placed our faith in our belief in this "very solid edifice," which turned out to be nothing more than a figment of our imagination—with hindsight, a catastrophic expression of our hubris.

Greenspan also said,

> The best minds at the Fed—including his own—could not have foreseen the explosion of subprime lending or the historic meltdown of the real-estate market...we're not smart enough as people...We just cannot see events that far in advance. And unless we can, it's very difficult to look back and say, "Why didn't we catch something?"[23]

Indeed, and it is just this lesson in which we all need to be schooled over and over again. We're just not smart enough—government officials, bankers, heads of corporations and other large institutions included. We build organizations sufficiently large and complex that we ourselves cannot understand them; it is inevitable that parts of those organizations will fail at some point in time for lack of oversight, and it is all too

---

[23] McKenna, "Greenspan admits 'mistake' on bank regulation."

41

possible that with poor governance born of our human limitations, the parts may consume the whole...lessons in humility.

Wednesday, November 05, 2008:
Reflections on Defiance and Subservience by GaveKal; on Servant Leadership and Hope by Loader

Obama is in; "change has come to America."[24] The markets are tentative, but I cast my vote for hope as captured in this paragraph from GaveKal today:

> The good news is—the Bush years are over. The other good news is that the election of a black president is in and of itself a triumph for America. If this historic event infuses Americans with pride, the country will enjoy an intangible dividend—the lifting of its collective spirits. Such dividends can have sweeping economic effects—imagine if the current environment of fear and malaise was miraculously replaced by one of American-style can-do confidence?[25]

If you want to assume a defeatist attitude, GaveKal offers the following:

> Others in the office, like Louis, Charles, Steve, Pierre...are more glum, fearing that President Obama's vision of the role of government is far closer to that of a European politician. Indeed, with a focus on a "right to healthcare" and a "right to housing" and a "right to clean air," Obama inverts the great idea of America as a republic whose government is restrained and limited by the natural rights of the individual, and replaces it with

---

[24] From President-elect Barack Obama's victory speech delivered November 5, 2008 (Chicago): "It's been a long time coming, but tonight, because of what we did on this date in this election at this defining moment, change has come to America."

[25] "Checking the Boxes: Wednesday, November 5, 2008," GaveKal Research (A GaveKal Limited Publication, November 5, 2008). GaveKal is a financial services, economic research and advisory firm with headquarters in Hong Kong and offices in the US, Europe and China.

a conventionally European view in which "rights" are granted by the state and devolved down to its citizens. In the first case, citizens always stand in defiance to the state (a stance which Louis and Charles find healthy), in the other, citizens stand in subservience to the state (the beginning of The Road to Serfdom?).[26]

GaveKal accurately identifies the tension between "defiance" and "subservience" that exists not only in relation to forms of government of the people but that pervades all working systems and relationships. If these states are understood by system participants to be in simple opposition to each other, the result is a win/lose mindset that dooms the system as a whole to sub-optimal results (like those we are experiencing today, into the second term of the Obama administration). Neither "defiance" nor "subservience" alone is the appropriate attitude between system participants striving for superior rewards. Why must we settle for only two options? There is a third; it's called "servant leadership," and by combining the best elements of defiance and subservience it really is a more workable long-term platform. Outwardly more naive, "reciprocal servant leadership" (from leaders to people and from people to leaders) extracts a greater short-term price and assumes more short-term risk, but with greater long-term certainty it delivers, with all of its blemishes, the greater reward. And need I point out that at the heart of servant leadership is a strong and healthy skepticism?

Monday, January 05, 2009:
A Very Insightful Comment on "Trust" from Tim Price, Director of Investment, PFP Wealth Management

Not just investment success, but the ability to sustain economic, government or life systems relies on trust between participants in the system. Tim Price understands the fragility of our systems and wonders where we're headed as trust is eroded:

From a year for markets that has already entered the history books, the Kerviel and Madoff scandals also highlight some

---

[26] "Checking the Boxes: Wednesday, November 5, 2008."

central aspects of the financial crisis. Trust as a commodity is increasingly hard to come by. As Michael Lewis and David Einhorn point out, the pertinent issue was how little interest anyone inside the financial system had in exposing such stupendous levels of fraud: "The fixable problem isn't the greed of the few but the misaligned interests of the many." And the sheer scale of the fraud involved—a scale matched only by the enormity of the financial bailouts from western governments—gives rise to a lingering uncertainty about the value of money in the first place. If so much money can be stolen (or distributed by government fiat, for that matter) with such apparent ease, what is that money really worth?[27]

Friday, January 30, 2009:
George Soros, Philosopher, Humanitarian, Skeptic, on His Theory of Reflexivity; Practical Implications of the Skeptical and Humble Mindset

Some years ago I read a biography written by George Soros. The book was entitled *Soros on Soros*.[28] I remember most Mr. Soros' humility as he makes a point of reminding us that his philanthropic initiatives only surfaced after he had made his first $25 million. In the book, he refers to himself as a "failed philosopher," as at the time his ideas were not widely accepted. Here again though, Chrystia Freeland gives us more insight into Mr. Soros' philosophical mindset, his skepticism, first of his own ideas, and his humility.

> George Soros' core idea is "reflexivity," which he defines as a "two-way feedback loop," between the participants' views and the actual state of affairs. People base their decisions not on the actual situation that confronts them, but on their perception or interpretation of the situation. Their decisions make an impact on the situation and changes in the situation are liable to change their perceptions.

---

[27] Tim Price, "Farewell to all that," PFP Wealth Management (London: January 5, 2009). Available at http://www.pfpg.co.uk/cms/document/Farewell_to_all_that.pdf.

[28] George Soros, *Soros on Soros: Staying Ahead of the Curve* (New York: Wiley, 1995).

It is, at its root, a case for frequent re-examination of one's assumptions about the world and for a readiness to spot and exploit moments of cataclysmic change—those times when our perceptions of events, and events themselves, are likely to interact most fiercely. It is also at odds with the rational expectations economic school, which has been the prevailing orthodoxy in recent decades. That approach assumed that economic players—from people buying homes to bankers buying subprime mortgages for their portfolios—were rational actors making, in aggregate, the best choices for themselves and that free markets were effective mechanisms for balancing supply and demand, setting prices correctly and tending towards equilibrium.

The rational expectations theory has taken a beating over the past 18 months: its intellectual nadir was probably October 23, 2008, when Alan Greenspan, the former Federal Reserve chairman, admitted to Congress that there was "a flaw in the model." Soros argues that the "market fundamentalism" of Greenspan and his ilk, especially their assumption that "financial markets are self-correcting," was an important cause of the current crisis. It befuddled policy-makers and was the intellectual basis for the "various synthetic instruments and valuation models," which contributed mightily to the crash.

Soros denies any great degree of emotional self-control; "That's not true, that's not true," he told me, shaking his head and smiling. "I am very emotional. I am as moody as the market, so I'm basically a manic depressive personality." (His market-linked moodiness extends to psychosomatic ailments, especially backaches, which he treats as valuable investment tips.) Instead, Soros attributes his effectiveness as an investor to his philosophical views about the contingent nature of human knowledge: "I think that my conceptual framework, which basically emphasises the importance of misconceptions, makes me extremely critical of my own decisions ... I know that I am bound to be wrong, and therefore am more likely to correct my own mistakes."[29]

As we wrap our heads around Soros' theory of "reflexivity" we understand that it implies a state of perpetual humility, born of the skeptical mindset.

Friday, February 06, 2009:
Ray Dalio Draws Parallels to Soros' Theory of Reflexivity and Reflects on the Importance of Character, Honesty, and "Client First" Values as Criterion for Selecting Your Investment Managers

Albeit a generalization, Ray Dalio has captured the culture of the investment industry very effectively in the following piece.

It seems to me that, above all else, what happened last year reflected human nature. No exogenous shocks caused what happened. The crisis was completely caused by people operating in a manner consistent with their individual natures and together in ways typical of group dynamics. In other words, people caused their circumstances, which they reacted to, which caused new circumstances that they reacted to, and so on. And they did this in ways that weren't very complex or unique...Speaking of human nature, greed, and fear, I want to say a few words about character, because I believe it also played a big role in determining investors' results and economic conditions in 2008, and that looking at how people acted can provide valuable lessons for the future. The greed that led to the bust was not just in the form of investors buying assets at high prices on leverage and driving risk premiums way down. It also came in the form of many investment managers who put making money for themselves ahead of doing what was best for their clients. This urge to make as much money as possible as fast as possible manifested itself in a range of ways and degrees,

---

[29] Chrystia Freeland, "The Credit Crunch According to Soros," *Financial Times* (January 30, 2009).

from downright cheating (e.g., in the case of Bernie Madoff), which happened in a small minority of cases, to being careless and not completely honest, which happened in the majority of cases. For example, I believe investment managers commonly slapped together tantalizing, unreliable investment products and described them to clients in less than totally accurate ways. And I believe that many investors naively didn't perceive this deception or they accepted it as a reality that they had to try to protect themselves against while investing with these people. In any case, investors commonly dealt with some managers whose character wasn't at a high enough level. *So, I believe that another important lesson should be to weigh character heavily in deciding whom to associate with. Just as you look at the length and quality of performance, look at the length and track record of character* [italics mine]. In the investment business, there are both wonderful and terrible people, and everything in between, so character should be at least as important a factor in choosing your investment managers as past investment performance.[30]

Dalio highlights the weaknesses inherent in our "human nature," the widespread habit of putting "making money for themselves ahead of doing what was best for their clients," the age of product proliferation wherein "investment managers commonly slapped together tantalizing, unreliable investment products and described them to clients in less than totally accurate ways," and from all of this he draws the lesson that we should "weigh character heavily in deciding whom to associate with."

Thursday, February 19, 2009:
John R. Taylor Jr. Reflects on "How Little All of Us Know"
Reaffirming my passion for the skeptical and the humble, John R. Taylor, chief investment officer at FX Concepts, comments as follows:

---

[30] Ray Dalio, "A note from Ray Dalio on 2008," Bridgewater Associates (Westport, 2008).

It is absolutely clear the US financial leaders Bernanke, Summers, Geithner, and Volcker are all in uncharted waters and they cannot see the hidden reefs and sandbars until the economy is upon them. Only Volcker gives the impression he is aware of how little all of us know about handling a globally inter-connected highly levered financial behemoth in this situation…Furthermore, the range of results in the real world is very wide, meaning our assumptions of normality are false, as the experience of October 1987 and October 1998 should have taught us. Basically, no one can forecast worth a damn.[31]

John Taylor's remarks are clear enough—no one can forecast worth a damn! If this is so, I wonder why we don't follow Jim Collins' now well-worn advice that maintains that we should grow up and "Confront the Brutal Facts"[32] by acknowledging and acting as though we can't forecast with any certainty. Doing so will help us stay the course—ever skeptical, ever humble!

Monday, January 19, 2009:
Received a Piece from Friends at Epoch Today and Responded

Importantly, Epoch's article addresses the moral vacuum today, more obvious than ever within the investment industry and broader society as well.[33] It advocates transparency through public listing and regulatory responsiveness as an essential element of the fuller solution. The article also discusses the more critical issues of leadership, character, integrity, trust and motivation, but as I argue, it gives these issues inadequate emphasis.

---

[31] John R. Taylor Jr., "Market Insight Report: Hitting the Broad Side of A Barn," *FX Concepts* (2009).

[32] Jim Collins, *Good to Great.*

[33] William W. Priest, "Sunlight and Transparency," *EPOCH Investment Partners* (January 2009). Priest is the CEO/CIO. The complete article is accessible at http://www.eipny.com/assets/pdfs/sunlight-and-transparency-01–01–2009.pdf.

Phil,

I enjoyed this piece immensely; since you have invited comment, may I say the following?

First, the article highlights several truths, but in my experience, places too much emphasis on the importance of public status and on reliance on external bodies for accountability. Much more important, I think, is the following point also made in the article: "a successful investment firm is managed not from the office of the CEO or CFO, but from the office of Compliance. It begins with a demand from the firm by its leadership to the individual employee that his or her conduct must be unimpeachable: a demand that must be backed up by an ethical code of conduct signed by every employee. The penalty for non-adherence is job termination."

This point stresses that the origination of essential core values is internal, i.e. internal to the organization, but more importantly, internal to the founding partners or leaders themselves. Accountability is thus driven by an independent office of compliance and potentially as well, by an independent member(s) of the board.

Proof of my point is all too easy today as we cast about the wreckage of so many public companies whose externally regulated transparency standards failed spectacularly to inhibit the unethical practices of the leadership (and armies of willing followers) of these public institutions.

Second, of course, the solution to this transparency issue lies in good measure with the clients themselves who, as the article states, must "want to know not only about the manager's investment philosophy and process, but about the manager him or herself. Who are these people? What is their character? What are their credentials? What motivates them? Are our interests and their interests aligned?" Trust must be the foundation of an investment relationship, but as Ronald Reagan noted, "verification is required," i.e., there must be substantive evidence to justify that trust.

Ralph

Again, this exchange posits integrity, core values, leadership and character as integral to better investment management and advocates diligence on the part of the client in seeking answers to these issues, which define investment excellence.

And four years after the onset of the crisis the drama continued, truth still evading us.

Thursday, April 14, 2011:
Global Financial Systems Are Built on Flawed Value Systems that Persist Today

In a quote from *Reuters*, Kevin Drawbaugh says:

> In the most damning official U.S. report yet produced on Wall Street's role in the financial crisis, a Senate panel accused power-house Goldman Sachs of misleading clients and manipulating markets, while also condemning greed, weak regulation and conflicts of interest throughout the financial system…"It shows without a doubt the lack of ethics in some of our financial institutions who embraced known conflicts of interest to accomplish wealth for themselves, not caring about the outcome for their customers," (said Republican Senator Tom Coburn).[34]

Monday, April 18, 2011:
Financial System a Ponzi Scheme?

In the following quotation Mariska van der Westen of Investments and Pensions Europe shows us how some, including former presidential adviser Larry Kotlikoff, believe that it is not only the value systems of the people engaged in the global financial system but the structural foundations of the system itself that are flawed and fraudulent. On that point this author reserves judgment and maintains hope that with all of their flaws, our financial and banking systems can be made to work to support the economic growth that is essential to the improved social well-being of all people.

---

[34] Kevin Drawbaugh, "Senate Panel Slams Goldman in Scathing Crisis Report," *Reuters* (April 13, 2011).

The world's financial system—which came spectacularly close to collapse with the fall of Lehman Brothers and the bailout of insurance giant AIG—is in essence a Ponzi scheme, according to Larry Kotlikoff, professor of economics at Boston University and former adviser to the president of the US.

"The system is a con game, characterised by a pervasive lack of transparency and made up of fraudulent guarantees and financial promises that cannot be kept," Kotlikoff said.

"The US government bailout has not solved the problem—on the contrary. AIG insured the uninsurable, and now the US government has taken over that role," Kotlikoff said. "But managing the crisis by taking on promises you can't deliver is not a fix to systemic risk. It is itself systemic risk."[35]

We have a few themes running through the writings of these highly respected people, but they overlap consistently and they are easily summarized as in the following table. Consider my summary; see if you agree with me about the prevalent themes. If you don't, read the articles again, and if you still don't agree with me, call me and let's talk it over. Here are the central ideas that these writers espouse for better results in your investment program, or in your life:

GFC Lessons from the Best and Brightest

Comment	Message	Central Theme
Greenspan: "We're not smart enough as people."	Humility	Core Values
GaveKal: identifies the hope in a new administration and the tension between "defiance" and "subservience."	Hope	Leadership

---

[35] Mariska van der Westen, "Financial System a Ponzi Scheme, Says Former Presidential Adviser Kotlikoff," *Investments & Pensions Europe* (April 18, 2011).

Comment	Message	Central Theme
Loader: "There is a third; it's called 'servant leadership.'"	Servant leadership	Leadership, core values
Tim Price: "Trust as a commodity is increasingly hard to come by…the misaligned interests of the many."	Trust	Core values
George Soros' Theory of Reflexivity: "I know that I am bound to be wrong, and therefore am more likely to correct my own mistakes."	Humility	Core values
Ray Dalio on 2008: "What happened last year reflected human nature; managers who put making money for themselves ahead of doing what was best for their clients; an important lesson should be to weigh character heavily in deciding whom to associate with."	Character, trust	Leadership, core values
John R. Taylor Jr.: "Basically, no one can forecast worth a damn."	Humility	Core values
Epoch: "Leadership…conduct must be unimpeachable; backed up by an ethical code of conduct…know about the manager him or herself."	Leadership, integrity, ethics, character, diligence	Leadership, core values
Tom Coburn: "Ethics in our financial institutions…not caring about the outcome for their customers."	Ethics, caring, alignment of interests	Core values
Larry Kotlikoff: "The world's financial system…is in essence a Ponzi scheme."	Acknowledging our limitations, humility	Core values, leadership

This table rounds out my effort to consolidate the ideas of a number of the investment world's thought leaders into a framework for actionable decisions. Our central themes are now evident; they are: 1) core values and 2) leadership, which together define the essential culture of an institution or, collectively, of the industry that any number of similar institutions comprise. How then do we build on these central themes to create the sound and durable culture and the essential operating framework that will yield more effective investment decision making in a better investment world?

In the next chapter, I begin to answer this question, but be cautioned that our discussion shifts gears somewhat. To this point we have addressed the investment industry at large, and indeed I even suggest that our lessons are transferable more broadly to all business and social institutions—for that matter, to life itself! The next three chapters are more narrowly focused; they derive from my research and experiences working with large institutional investors, and the lessons apply most directly to boards of directors, pension and investment committees and managers of pension plans, endowments and foundations although important extrapolations of many of our ideas may still be made to a broader constituency. As promised in this book's introductory chapter, I return to higher level and life-specific issues in the final three chapters of my story. There I speak to the largely unseen link between investment excellence (governance, policy and risk management), i.e., "money," and "faith." You will recall from chapter 1 that my original mission was centred on money. But on the road to money, I encountered faith and have understood faith as the far more valuable pursuit.

CHAPTER 5

Governance (G)

Committee Woes:
"O give me your pity, I'm on a committee
Which means that from morning to night,
We attend and amend, and contend and defend
Without a conclusion in sight.
We confer and concur, we defer and demur
And reiterate all of our thoughts.
We revise the agenda with frequent addenda,
And consider a load of reports.
We compose and propose, we suppose and oppose,
And the points of procedure are fun;
But though various notions are brought up as motions,
There's terribly little gets done.
We resolve and absolve, but we never dissolve,
Since it's out of the question for us.
What a shattering pity to end our committee.
Where else could we make such a fuss?"
Posted by Merrill Cook at note 10974 of Pnet Chat,
a meeting on PresbyNet, the PCUSA electronic bulletin board

THE ONSET OF THE NEW MILLENNIUM HAS BROUGHT WITH IT MEANING-
ful advances in our understanding of the link between studied
investment governance and better investment outcomes. Much

has been written and contributions to the educational process have been made by many. In this chapter, I dissect for their essence the findings of four major contributors to the process—Paul Myners (UK),[36] Keith Ambachtsheer (Canada),[37] Professor Gordon L. Clark[38]

---

[36] Paul Myners, CBE (born 1 April 1948), was the financial services secretary (sometimes referred to as city minister) in HM Treasury, the UK's finance ministry, during the Labour government of Gordon Brown. He held the position from October 2008 until May 2010 and was made a life peer in consequence of his appointment, as he was not an elected Member of Parliament. He also served on the prime minister's national economic council. Myners has worked in the financial sector since 1974. He has also held a number of third sector posts, including chairman of the Trustees of Tate and chairman of the Low Pay Commission, all of which he relinquished on his ministerial appointment. Immediately prior to his ministerial appointment he was chairman of the Guardian Media Group, publisher of *The Guardian* and *The Observer* newspapers, and chairman of Land Securities Group, the largest quoted property company in Europe at that time. He is a former chairman of Marks & Spencer and deputy chairman of PowerGen. More at http://en.wikipedia.org/wiki/Paul_Myners,_Baron_Myners.

[37] Keith Ambachtsheer has been a participant in the pensions and investments industry since 1969. He founded his own firm, KPA Advisory Services, in 1985. Through it, he provides strategic advice to a global clientele in person and through the monthly *Ambachtsheer Letter*. He is the author of three best-selling books, and has been a regular contributor to industry publications since the 1970s. He is the publisher and editor of the new Rotman International Journal of Pension Management, which launched in October 2008. Having played a major role in founding the Rotman International Centre for Pension Management (Rotman ICPM), he was appointed director of Rotman ICPM and adjunct professor of finance at the Rotman School of Management, University of Toronto in April 2005. From http://webcast.streamlogics.com/customer/tdsecurities/online-forms/2009Sep11_1/auditorium/resources/ambachtsheer_bio_website.pdf.

[38] Gordon L Clark DSc (Oxon) FBA is the Halford Mackinder Professor of Geography at Oxford University andholds a professorial fellowship at St Peter's College. Previous academic appointments have been at Harvard Law School, Harvard's Kennedy School of Government, the University of Chicago, Carnegie Mellon's Heinz School and Monash University. An economic geographer with an abiding interest in the tension between global financial integration and national and regional institutions, his research has a number of related strands. One is focused on global finance and the investment management industry, including the governance structure and decision-making performance of pension funds, endowments, and sovereign wealth funds. Papers on this topic have been published in the *Journal of Pension Economics and Finance* (2004, 2006, 2007), the *Rotman International Journal of Pension Management* (2008, 2010), the *Journal of Asset Management* (2008), *Risk Management and Insurance Review* (2009), and *Pensions: An International Journal* (2010). From http://www.sirp.se/web/page.aspx?refid=683.

and Roger Urwin (UK).[39]

Myners

In 2001, after 27 years work in the financial services sector, the last 13 years as chairman of the Gartmore Group, Paul Myners retired from Gartmore to pursue wider interests, which included a documented review of institutional investment in the United Kingdom, prepared for Gordon Brown, then chancellor of the exchequer, HM Treasury, United Kingdom.[40] Myners' work succeeded in raising the ire of many of his former industry colleagues as he tackled long-standing practices and conflicts that had served industry participants well, its clients less so. The scope of Myners' work is much broader than the immediate concerns of this book, but his efforts lay bare several of the major failings of pension fund governance in the UK. Not surprisingly, the North American pension fund community struggles with these same governance challenges, and so they are highlighted here. Given our intended space allocation to this subject we can do no better than to present Paul Myners' own summary of his recommended governance principles for defined benefits pension schemes. Myners himself notes that "these principles might appear basic, but the review believes" (and I would concur) "that they call for considerable change in pension fund practice." In summary form, the main points of Myners' principles for defined benefits pension schemes are as follows:

---

[39] Roger Urwin is the global head of investment content for Towers Watson, a post he assumed in July 2008 after acting as the global head of the investment practice from 1995 to 2008. Urwin joined Watson Wyatt in 1989 to start the firm's investment consulting practice, and under his leadership the practice grew to a global team of 500. His prior career involved heading the Mercer investment practice and leading the business development and quantitative investment functions at Gartmore Investment Management. Urwin has a degree in mathematics from Oxford University and a master's in applied statistics also from Oxford. He qualified as a fellow of the Institute of Actuaries in 1983. From http://events.towerswatson.com/events/tool/render.asp?evtid=15731&country=australia&page=3&bio=speaker15146&isapi=on&lang=en-AU.

[40] Paul Myners, "Institutional Investment in the United Kingdom," HM Treasury & The Department for Work and Pensions (March 2001).

Principles

- Decisions should be taken only by persons or organisations with the right skills, information and resources needed to take them effectively.
- Trustees should set out an overall investment objective for the fund, in terms which relate directly to the circumstances of the fund and not to some other objective such as the performance of other pension funds.
- The attention devoted to asset allocation decisions should fully reflect the contribution they can make to achieving the fund's investment objective.
- Decision-makers should consider a full range of investment opportunities across all major asset classes, including private equity.
- The fund should be prepared to pay sufficient fees for actuarial and investment advice to attract a broad range of kinds of potential providers.
- Trustees should give fund managers an explicit written mandate setting out the agreement between them on issues such as the investment objective, and a clear timescale for measurement and evaluation.
- In consultation with their investment manager, funds should explicitly consider whether the index benchmarks that they have selected are appropriate. Where they believe active management to have the potential to achieve higher returns, they should set both targets and risk controls that reflect this, allowing sufficient freedom for genuinely active management to occur.
- Trustees should arrange to measure the performance of the fund and the effectiveness of their own decision-making, and formally to assess the performance and decision-making delegated to advisers and managers.[41]

In December 2004, HM Treasury, following the conclusion of its review into how effective Myners' principles had been in improving pension schemes' investment decision-making, announced proposals to strengthen Myners' principles. In its 45-page report, the treasury noted the efforts that pension schemes were making to adopt Myners'

---

[41] Myners, "Institutional Investment in the United Kingdom," 15.

principles but concluded that further action was needed, in particular in relation to trustee expertise and the decision-making processes.

The main proposals were:

- The chairman of the trustee board should be responsible for ensuring that trustees taking investment decisions are familiar with investment issues and that the board has sufficient trustees for that purpose;
- In the case of funds with more than 5,000 members:
  - the chairman of the trustee board and at least one-third of trustees should be familiar with investment issues (even where investment decisions have been delegated to an investment sub-committee); and
  - there should be access to in-house investment expertise equivalent at least to one full-time staff member familiar with investment issues.
- In relation to investment advice, as well as contracting separately for investment and actuarial advice (as currently), funds should also contract separately for strategic asset allocation and fund manager selection advice.
- Trustees should provide the results of monitoring of their own performance to members, and ensure that key information provided to members is also available on a dedicated fund website.[42]

Ambachtsheer

In 2005, Ambachtsheer, Capelle and Lum produced a research progress report wherein they noted that some of the earliest contributions to pension fund governance included Peter Drucker's *The Unseen Revolution* (1976), Ambachtsheer's own *Pension Funds and the Bottom Line* (1985), and O'Barr and Conley's *Folly and Fortune* (1992).[43]

In 2007, Ambachtsheer, Capelle and Lum analyzed and reported the findings of a survey of senior pension fund executives on pension fund

---

[42] Taken from "Myners' Principles for Institutional Investment Decision-Making: Review of Progress," HM Treasury (December 2004).

[43] Keith Ambachtsheer, Ronald Capelle, and Hubert Lum, "The Pension Fund Governance Deficit: Still With Us," *Rotman International Journal of Pension Management*, vol. 1, issue 1 (Fall 2008), 14–21.

governance. The authors comment on the paucity of empirical research pertaining to pension fund governance and the resulting considerable knowledge gaps. The report classifies survey responses to identify the following four overriding areas of specific challenge, each subclassified for further clarity:

1. Agency/context issues
   a) Balancing stakeholder interests
   b) Understanding the legal/regulatory environment
2. Oversight effectiveness issues
   a) Appropriate skill/knowledge set for the Board
   b) Clear delegation to management
3. Investment beliefs/risk management issues
   a) Understanding context-based risk and its management
   b) Informed 'investment beliefs' and their relevance
   c) Shift to risk budget-based investment process
4. Strategic planning/management effectiveness issues
   a) Resource planning, organization design, and compensation
   b) Clear delegation from the Board
   c) Effective IT-based implementation systems

The study suggests the following five opportunities to improve pension fund governance and it argues for pension regulators to require that pension funds disclose on a regular basis what steps they are taking in the five listed governance improvement opportunity areas:

- Redesign pension deals to eliminate the 'competing financial interests' problem
- Develop templates for ideal boards of governors composition, and integrate these templates into actual selection processes
- Initiate board effectiveness self-evaluation processes
- Achieve clarity between the respective roles of boards and management
- Adopt high-performance cultures with competitive compensation policies.[44]

---

[44] Ambachtsheer, Capelle, and Lum, "The Pension Fund Governance Deficit: Still With Us," 14–21.

Clark and Urwin

Later in 2007, Clark and Urwin published the results of their own research based on detailed qualitative discussions with ten funds from around the world (ranging in size from $5 billion to $100 billion) that had built reputations for excellent governance and had delivered strong performance in addition.[45] They defined three types of fund structure/ organizational design, ranging from very simple (type 1) to very sophisticated (type 3), and they identified 12 "best-practice" governance factors.[46] The authors then organized these factors according to their relevance (or achievability) to each of their three defined fund structure types. They summarize their findings in the following tables:

The 12 Factor Model of Best-Practice[47]

Core Best-Practice Factors *Relevant to all funds, especially type 1 and 2 funds*	
Mission clarity	Clarity of the mission and the commitment of stakeholders to the mission statement
Effective focusing of time	Resourcing each element in the investment process with an appropriate budget considering impact and required capabilities
Leadership	Leadership, being evident at the board / investment committee level, with the key role being the investment committee chairman

---

[45] Gordon L Clark and Roger Urwin, "Best-Practice Investment Management: Lessons for Asset Owners from the Oxford–Watson Wyatt Project on Governance," October 2007.

[46] Clark and Urwin, "Best-Practice Investment Management," 19: The simplest type (type 1) is a system of collective deliberation wherein the board makes decisions on a routine basis with the support of a consultant and external service providers. A more sophisticated version utilizes an investment committee subject to the final approval at the board relying, again, on collective decision-making according to the regular meeting schedule (type 2). Type 3 employs in-house investment expertise as a key factor in best-practice to drive real-time decision-making.

[47] Clark and Urwin, "Best-Practice Investment Management," 18.

Strong beliefs	Strong investment beliefs commanding fund-wide support that align with goals and inform all investment decision-making
Risk budget framework	Frame the investment process by reference to a risk budget aligned to goals and incorporating an accurate view of alpha and beta
Fit-for-purpose manager line-up	The effective use of external managers, governed by clear mandates, aligned to goals, selected on fit for purpose criteria

Exceptional best-practice factors
Relevant only to type 3 funds

Investment executive	The use of a highly investment competent investment function tasked with clearly specified responsibilities, with clear accountabilities to the investment committee
Required competencies	Selection to the board and senior staff guided by: numeric skills, capacity for logical thinking, ability to think about risk in the probability domain
Effective compensation	Effective compensation practices used to build bench strength and align actions to the mission, different strategies working according to fund context
Competitive positioning	Frame the investment philosophy and process by reference to the institution's comparative advantages and disadvantages
Real-time decisions	Utilise decision-making systems that function in real-time not calendar-time
Learning organization	Work to a learning culture which deliberately encourages change and challenges the commonplace assumptions of the industry

Where's the Beef? Here's the Beef!

On the subject of pension fund governance, thanks to the authors of our selected research, we are given a lot to think about in the realm of what constitutes best practice. To render the results a little less daunting I have tried, with some success I think, to dissect these papers for what I consider their essence. In summary point form, then, the following are what I believe to be the essentials of best practice pension fund governance:

Six Simple Principles of Best Practice Pension Fund Governance

1. Mission clarity specific to the deliverable (i.e., liability driven) addressing agency/context issues by (as Ambachtsheer suggests) redefining the pension deal if and as necessary.
2. Clearly defined investment beliefs. Well worth mentioning here are Myners' reflections on the need to devote more resource to asset allocation policy, strategy and tactics. Myners is probably right about this as a potential source of incremental expected risk-adjusted return, but the resource devoted to asset allocation issues should reflect the board's (not Myners') relevant beliefs.
3. A clearly defined and demonstrably liability-aware risk management process.
4. Effective time and resource management achieved by the implementation of a planning and regular review process focusing on organizational design, and time and resource allocation. Such planning and review processes include the constant re-evaluation of the organization's real-time decision-making capability and its compensation and cost structures.
5. Effective **leadership** that assumes full responsibility for:
    a) populating board and executive with people well-skilled to perform the essential functions,
    b) ensuring the controlled delegation of all non-governance, non-policy (i.e., non-board) related functions to an internal executive or to external, qualified suppliers and confirming the full, clear and documented assignment of the authority required to perform delegated responsibilities,

c) encouraging a learning culture, guided by the organization's own core values,

d) overseeing a regular and rigorous self-evaluation (board and governance) process and

e) ensuring regular, effective and transparent reporting to all stakeholders.

6. **Core values** defined and documented.

So there we have it—six simple principles to best practice pension fund governance—the essentials of what I believe are a blueprint for a better investment world. Sound investment policies and effective risk management (the "P" and "R" of my GPR Model) are further essentials, and we deal with them in our next two chapters, but to be perfectly candid, policy and risk management are simply mechanics that flow rather naturally from the board's rigorously considered governance work. Getting governance right is very hard work; get the governance right, however, and with only a little more work the rest of the puzzle falls neatly into place. Ignoring any piece of the governance pie, however, risks a rude awakening, pie in face!

Notice if you will, the significance of our simple principle #5 (leadership) in the preceding list, significant by virtue of its volume in relation to the other five points. And notice simple principle #6 (core values), significant by virtue of the fact that as with the word "leadership" I used bold letters to bring your attention to it. These two principles, effective leadership and core values, correspond to the themes that we identified towards the end of chapter 4, themes that we said were central to the broader framework for actionable decisions that will yield better investment decisions in a better investment world. Two of the three studies that we used to review the essentials of sound pension fund governance posited the need for effective leadership, but not one of them addressed the importance of core values, so I feel compelled to explain something of my decision to stress core values and effective leadership as the two most important of the six simple principles.

Effective Leadership and Core Values—Inextricably Linked

For some years now I have been formulating this idea that no matter our line of endeavour, surely we need more leaders. The world, in fact, suffers from a serious dearth of leaders, and it's not hard to see why. Scratch beneath the surface of claims that "I wish I were running this place" and you find few people ready and willing to assume the leader's role, and for very good reason. People understand that leadership is tough; its struggles are many; its rewards are few! Thirty odd years in the business of studying investment management firms have convinced me that more than any other single issue, effective leadership will determine the future prospects of a given firm. Then there is the matter of definition; what do we mean by effective leadership? Charlie Ellis' book *Capital* and Jim Collins' book *Good to Great* and, finally, Jim Ware's book *Investment Leadership* all deal in different ways with the leadership issue. Great books, all of them, but Collins' book was most helpful for its work in drilling down to uncover the definition, the characteristics if you will, of effective leaders. I first learned of his book in 2002 when the Reverend Richard Topping at The Church of St. Andrew and St. Paul in Montreal announced one sunny Sunday morning that the day's sermon would be based on readings from *Harvard Business Review*! He caught my attention and then gave a synopsis of the article "Level 5 Leadership—The Triumph of Humility and Fierce Resolve" by Jim Collins, which appeared in the January 2001 edition of *Harvard Business Review*. The article effectively summarizes Collin's book (*Good to Great*), which documents the findings of five years of research conducted by a dedicated team committed to shedding light on the underlying drivers of sustained excellence in great companies. As you may guess from the title of the article, the simple answer is leadership. But less simple, and far more revealing, I believe, are the advances that Collins and his team of 21 researchers made in defining the term "leadership." This work teaches us that level 5 leadership—the kind of leadership that results in sustained greatness—is embodied in two character traits, namely, humility and resolve, quite contrary to conventional (media driven) wisdom, which would have us believe that our best leaders are those who project ego and charisma.

65

The implications of these findings are revolutionary! Collins' work points us to two primary drivers of effective leadership, humility and resolve. For Collins' purposes these drivers are "character traits;" for our purposes they become "core values" that are central to effective leadership. If, as we have already concluded, effective leadership is central to sound governance, the centrality of core values to sound governance is proven by deduction! In all, Collins' research cites six key concepts that work to propel a firm from good to great; all six, in one sense or another, are tied to core values.

Jim Ware's book *Investment Leadership* builds on this idea by addressing the special role that core values play within the investment business, a business founded on trust and dependent on trust (witness 2008) for its continued existence. An absolute must for every investment manager, investment consultant and plan sponsor, *Investment Leadership* is insightful, well-written and practical; it comes fully assembled and ready to apply to your day-to-day investment business management concerns. Thank you, Mr. Ware!

Ware makes the important point that to be effective values need to be (1) stated (by which he presumably also means documented), (2) defined, and (3) lived passionately.

There are three powerful benefits of values work:
1. Hiring and promoting decisions become easier.
2. Termination decisions become clearer.
3. Morale is improved as individuals de-select themselves from a team.[48]

He concludes that identity, in a nutshell, is what core values are all about: "When you know who you are, you don't sweat the small stuff. And you survive the big, hard stuff."[49]

To be sure, core values are no silver bullet; in the best of times they serve as a guide that inspires and influences all decision making and behaviour in relation to relevant stakeholders in the business (clients,

---

[48] Jim Ware, Beth Michaels, and Dale Primer, *Investment Leadership: Building a Winning Culture for Long-Term Success*, Wiley Finance 203 (Hoboken: John Wiley & Sons, 2004), 38.

[49] Ware, Michaels and Primer, *Investment Leadership*, 40.

colleagues, owners); in the worst of times they may serve as a check against people's worst behaviour by establishing ground rules that can be referenced when settling negotiations or ironing out disagreements. In real life, of course, there can be no guarantee that in the worst of times people will adhere to even the most clearly documented and carefully communicated core values. But as with investment choices, I prefer those with a greater probability of success, and clearly, at the price, a clearly documented, carefully communicated and passionately lived statement of core values is a very inexpensive hedge against the worst case scenario, with virtually no downside!

Document, Document, Document

A natural and healthy skepticism leads us to identify two central themes, leadership and core values, as essential to the creation of the sound and durable culture that we need for better investment decisions in a better investment world. Governance, we have said, is the forum for the embodiment of these two central themes and for the remaining four of our six simple principles. It may follow as self-evident, but experience has taught me, and I think it is worth stressing, the importance of not just "talking the governance talk" but also committing the talk to writing. Governance policies and principles must be documented and, need I say, must include a section outlining and defining the institution's core values if they are going to be understood, agreed to and acted upon by current and future stakeholders. Strangely, I think, pension regulatory bodies require the documentation of investment policies but have stopped short of requiring the documentation of the much more far-reaching and pertinent governance policies and principles. In my experience very few pension funds, for example, or government, corporate or non-profit bodies for that matter, have committed the resources required to fully contemplate, document and promote a sound governance structure uniquely tailored to the requirements of their own institution. And no wonder, for as we have already noted, "getting governance right is very hard work!" But that's no excuse, is it?

CHAPTER 6
Policy (P)

"What we call the beginning is often the end. And to make an end is to make a beginning. The end is where we start from."
T. S. Eliot
[In policy governance the beginning point for making a difference is indeed defining the ends, and defining ends is the beginning of better governance.]

ALTHOUGH INVESTMENT POLICIES AND RISK MANAGEMENT ARE DISTINCTLY part of the overall governance project, I have chosen to address each separately, to make in each case one or two key points regarding ideas that I believe must bear more importantly on our thinking as we introduce change to our traditional practices within these two disciplines.

Investment policy for institutional funds certainly is well attended. For decades now, by regulatory authority, pension funds have been required to document their investment policies, and formatting is reasonably standardized to incorporate a general statement of objectives, asset allocation guidelines and portfolio and security constraints. In light of the frequency and severity of market events over the past three decades, and having witnessed the implications of these events for the viability of long-established pension funds, plan sponsors, trustees and regulators are now sensitized to the limitations of the conventional statement of investment policies.

Investment Beliefs

In fact, the major shortcoming that I have observed with the typical statement of investment policies has nothing to do with the investment policies themselves. Rather, it has everything to do with the derivation of the thinking that precedes the creation of the investment policy statement. The thinking that forms the foundation for investment policies can only logically derive from key elements of the investment fund's governance structure, and as we have already noted, governance policies and principles are seldom documented. In fact, while ideas about governance are shared at the trustee level, governance practices are mostly creatures of habit subject to critical review infrequently, if at all. One result, for example, is that investment policies will be documented without sufficient attention to the fundamental investment beliefs of the trustees. If investment beliefs are not first carefully considered, documented and approved at the trustee level (simple governance principle #2), investment policies and the strategic decisions that flow from them will inevitably reflect inconsistencies throughout. A simple example arises when the majority of trustees on a given committee believe, implicitly or explicitly, that active management cannot add value in the most efficient markets, but for lack of consideration, documentation and formal approval of this belief, their ideas are not incorporated into the investment policy statement, and 75 percent of the U.S. Equity (an efficient market) portfolio remains actively managed with active management fees applicable—money lost inadvertently.

Funding Policy

At a higher level many "pension" committees are, from a governance perspective, constrained to responsibility for investment related matters **only**, i.e., they have no say with respect to liability related matters (benefits, funding, etc.). This misses the point that the pension plan (benefits structures, resulting liabilities, funding policies and investment policies) is one—a single entity—in which decisions relating to any part affect the whole. You simply can't set responsible investment policies without specific reference to benefits, liabilities and funding. Few investment policy statements that I have seen make any meaningful reference to liabilities, although many state broad generalizations that are at best unhelpful or more often and more seriously, misleading as to what is achievable through a well-managed investment program. CAPSA addressed this issue in a rather good consultation paper published in November 2009.[50] The paper considers numerous governance, funding and investment issues and renders sound recommendations throughout and in particular with respect to the need for careful and complete documentation of all policies, procedures, practices and decisions. On funding, for example, and its relationship to investment policies, CAPSA states the following:

> In Canada, minimum pension standards legislation requires plan administrators, as a rule, to adopt a statement of investment policies and procedures (SIP&P). Although it is not a requirement under any current pension legislation, it is a good practice and an integral part of the pension plan's governance structure, for plan sponsors of defined benefit pension plans to develop and adopt a funding policy.
>
> There are a number of advantages for developing a funding policy:
> - The exercise of developing a funding policy should improve the plan sponsor's and other parties' understanding of the risks involved and the factors that affect the variability of funding requirements and security of benefits. As a result, the plan sponsor should improve its identification and management of risks, which should lead to more robust governance.
> - The adoption of a funding policy could increase the plan sponsor's discipline around funding decisions. This could contribute to more stability in funding and reduce the risk of intervention by regulators.

---

[50] "The Prudence Standard and the Roles of the Plan Sponsor and Plan Administrator in Pension Plan Funding and Investment," Canadian Association of Pension Supervisory Authorities (November 30, 2009).

- Having a written summary of the funding policy that is accessible to plan members and beneficiaries will improve the transparency of funding decisions.
- Having a funding policy also provides guidance to the plan's actuary when he/she is selecting actuarial assumptions in accordance with actuarial standards of practice and within the plan sponsor's risk tolerance limits.

The specifics of the SIP&P should be considered when setting the funding policy. It is important to ensure that the two documents are consistent with each other and changes may be required to either the SIP&P or the funding policy to achieve consistency.[51]

In short, benefits policies, investment policies **and** funding policies work together to form a responsible plan, a clear mission (simple governance principle #1) for managing and meeting plan liabilities.

Outside the Box—Objectives, Guidelines, Constraints

Finally, as we review the relationship of various policy statements to each other and to the plan's overall governance principles, the opportunity presents itself to undertake a complete rethink of the methodology employed in the standard format for the expression of fund objectives, guidelines and constraints. "The essence of investment management," said legendary investor Benjamin Graham, "is the management of risks, not the management of returns."[52] A review of the subject matter of industry publications since 2008 suggests that we are beginning to see the wisdom of Ben Graham's reproof. More is being written on risk management, and, not surprisingly, risk management product offerings are no longer in short supply. A result of this increased activity around risk and risk management is heightened awareness of new methods for defining and managing risk, all of which bears importantly on the

---

[51] "The Prudence Standard and the Roles of the Plan Sponsor and Plan Administrator in Pension Plan Funding and Investment," 15.

[52] "Seeking Asymmetric Returns: Improving the Odds of Investment Success," Alliance-Bernstein (July 2011).

manner in which we choose to express fund objectives, guidelines and constraints.

Perhaps, as trustees, we need to bring fresh vision and a new mindset to our investment policy statements. Perhaps we need to concern ourselves more with the message that our stated objectives holds for the stakeholders of the plan. At the total fund level, our objective statements employ "benchmarks" that are constructed from widely accepted indices that are structurally biased in ways that probably bear no resemblance to our investment beliefs, whether implicit or explicit. We use these benchmarks to target objectives for rates-of-return, and portfolio risk guidelines or constraints relating to volatility or "tracking error" and sector and security allocations. What if, as Ben Graham suggests, we were to redirect our primary focus away from rates-of-return towards those measures of risk that best reflect our central mission? What if we were to break away altogether from the standard capital market indices and build our benchmarks from the bottom up, based strictly on our investment beliefs and driven by our mission? "Success" under this scenario would be measured in two parts, both ultimately impacting funding requirements and funded status:

1. in part by unexpected, positive or negative variance in asset values, and

2. in part by unexpected, positive or negative variance in our stated objectives, e.g. the liabilities related to our pension deal.

Risk is now calculated differently, portfolios are structured differently, investment managers are accountable only for the variance from their assigned benchmark, and trustees are accountable for the selection (or creation of) various benchmarks, for the policy weight assigned to those benchmarks and (unless otherwise delegated) for any deviation from assigned policy weights. Expanding on this idea, it becomes quickly evident that any positive or negative variances in asset values will be driven most importantly by trustee decisions, not by investment manager decisions.[53]

---

[53] Digressing momentarily, this naturally raises the question: "Why is it that investment managers are compensated so much more generously than trustees?" The answer to this very interesting question is unfortunately outside of the scope of this book, but the question is addressed at length in the works of Paul Myners and Keith Ambachtsheer.

The issue of appropriate choice and construction of benchmarks is an important one that deserves much more attention than we can devote to it here. Ron Surz has invested a lot of energy in this subject over a lot of years and he concludes quite logically, "The key to accurate insights is accurate benchmarking because if the benchmark is wrong all of the analytics are wrong."[54] Preferring customized benchmarks, he discourages the practice of settling for off-the-shelf indexes, because many managers are liberated from style boxes and because many off-the-shelf indices are not mutually exclusive and exhaustive in combination. Surz's primary concern is that benchmarks be so constructed as to enable the accurate measurement and separation of investment skill from investment style. My greater concern is that selected benchmarks accurately reflect trustee investment beliefs so that investment mandates are clearly defined and so that accountability for policy (strategic) decisions versus tactical decisions is properly assigned, understood and rewarded.

To conclude then on the matter of investment policies (by which we mean stated objectives, guidelines and constraints, even to the choice and construction of benchmarks), at the risk of being repetitive I will reiterate that the issue of overriding importance is not the content and format of the investment policies themselves. Rather, it is policy inconsistencies, i.e., the lack of careful policy integration with trustee investment beliefs, with implicit or explicitly stated funding policies and with the plan's central mission and measures of risk that best reflect that mission.

---

[54] Ronald J. Surz, "The New 'Trust but Verify,'" *Finweek* (March 18, 2010), 15. Surz is the president and CEO at PPCA, San Clemente.

CHAPTER 7

Risk (R)

"Not everything that counts can be counted,
and not everything that can be counted counts."
Sign hanging in Einstein's office at Princeton

THE FINANCIAL CRISIS OF 2008 WAS THE PROVERBIAL STRAW THAT BROKE the camel's back. It was the last in a series of too-closely timed "Black Swan" events that served to redirect institutional investor thought away from return expectations back to where, according to Ben Graham, it should have resided all along, namely, on risk management. In the short span of time since 2008 so much attention (both the spoken and written word) has been devoted to the subject of risk management that it is quite difficult to know at what point I should begin to unleash my monologue on you, particularly as I have earlier promised to restrict my expressed views and ideas on risk management to one or two key points. Perhaps it will be easiest to attack this problem, once again, from the point of view of the skeptic. Let's first consider what to look out for—pitfalls to avoid in the arena of risk management. In a word, or rather in a title, I will subtitle this section "Never Marry a Model," giving full credit for the witticism to one of my esteemed colleagues, Bob Collie at Russell Investments, who presented a very balanced assessment of the utility of modelling for strategic and tactical investment decision-making purposes in a paper entitled "Don't Marry a Model," delivered in February 2011.

Bob opens his paper by noting,

> We build models all the time: on computers, on paper, out of physical materials or just in our heads. Often we are not even aware that we're doing so. But whether it's a simple analogy we're making, or a particular perspective we're bringing to a question we face, there's a "model"—a simplified representation of reality—behind just about every decision we make.[55]

He continues by citing George E. P. Box's observation "All models are wrong, but some are useful,"[56] and he concludes with his own straightforward admonition: "Models should serve as an aid to understanding and not a replacement for it."[57]

Once again, it is in the reasonable skepticism around conventional approaches to problem solving, demonstrated by people like Bob Collie, that I find hope that over time, we may actually improve our problem-solving capabilities.

A year or so after the Crisis of 2008, I found myself freed of corporate obligations for the first time in my adult life, and I set out on a research sabbatical to satisfy my personal curiosity about what I perceived as gross inadequacies in the management of risk for institutional funds. As far back as the late '70s, early '80s, pension funds were shedding the "balanced fund" approach to asset management in favour of specialist managers. Somewhere in the transition phase, the essence of asset allocation and risk management was allowed to fall between the cracks, and later the cracks were papered over with claims regarding the ineffectiveness of market timing and the wisdom of rebalancing to fixed asset allocation policies and with a misguided move to index-based "benchmarking" to replicate selected asset classes. Nice ideas in a "Gaussian" world,

---

[55] Bob Collie, "Don't Marry a Model," *Viewpoint: Russell Research* (Russell Investments, February 2011), 1. Collie is FIA, chief research strategist, Americas Institutional.

[56] Collie, "Don't Marry a Model," 1, citing George E. P. Box and Norman R. Draper, *Empirical Model-Building and Response Surfaces*, Wiley Series in Probability and Statistics (New York: Wiley, 1987).

[57] Collie, "Don't Marry a Model," 9.

but if it was not evident before, it is surely evident now that we do not live in a Gaussian world. Fat tails (i.e. extreme events) do prevail and will be ignored at our peril! How then, I wondered, can we deal with this new reality, what Bill Gross calls the "new normal"?[58] Surely, I thought, there exist some very smart people who have developed a model capable of capturing the unique attributes of a given pension/ endowment/foundation fund and matching those attributes against a likely range of capital market expectations in a manner that allows us to establish and manage a total portfolio risk profile sensibly tailored to the institutional investor's unique objectives and risk tolerance. In the sense of the single model that I had dreamed of, my research, of course, uncovered none. The time was ripe for Liability Driven Investing (LDI) by many definitions, and asset management firms were aggressively seeking entrée into this pension planning space by offering strategic services contingent upon client commitment to the firm's higher-profile investment products (mostly fixed income, swaps or derivatives trading based) to achieve client-specific risk management objectives. Close, but as we say in the business, "no cigar!"

Before I press on with this story, some clarification as to the term "Gaussian" will be helpful to ensure that we are pressing on together. In probability theory, the *normal* (or Gaussian) distribution is a continuous probability distribution that is often used as a first approximation to describe real-valued random variables that tend to cluster around a single mean value. The graph of the associated probability density function is "bell"-shaped or "normally" distributed and is known as the Gaussian function or bell curve to acknowledge the thought leadership in this discipline of the German mathematician and scientist Johann Carl Friedrich Gauss. Hence, a "Gaussian" mindset simply implies the assumption that **normally** distributed events (the bell-shaped curve) adequately describe probabilities for future outcomes in the world in which we live.

---

[58] The idea of a "new normal" is discussed in Mohamed A. El-Erian, William H. Gross, "Mohamed El-Erian and Bill Gross Discuss PIMCO's Cyclical Outlook and the New Normal," *Economic Outlook* (PIMCO, October 2009). PIMCO's new normal is a world in which growth prospects may be lower and long-held assumptions about portfolio allocations are challenged.

Carl Friedrich Gauss (1777-1855)
Painted by Christian Albrecht Jensen

Partway through my two-year research sabbatical I met a man whose grasp of the mathematics of finance, natural skepticism, humility and sense of humour won me over to his particular point of view with remarkably little resistance on my own part. The man's name is Jim Otar; he is from Turkey and has retained enough of an accent to, together with his frizzy-haired appearance and his over-sized spectacles, render his arguments highly persuasive. Jim is a financial planner who works out of his own home north of Toronto and travels extensively to present at workshops on non-Gaussian retirement planning. He holds a master of engineering degree from the University of Toronto; he has written several books and over 100 articles on advanced retirement planning and market history; he builds retirement planning models with a passion I have seldom witnessed anywhere and has thus "played with the numbers" long enough to understand them well. His work on the devastating effects of the sequence of returns, market cycles, the luck factor and the time value of fluctuations has won him writing and research rewards. Jim's ideas on these matters are enlightening, even fascinating. Since I can't possibly capture them all here, I offer my endorsement of his book *Unveiling the Retirement Myth* and, per the following quotes from his book, Jim's thoughts on the application of modelling processes that flow from the "Gaussian mindset" to the challenges of retirement planning:[59]

Jim C. Otar (1951 -)
CFP, CMT, BASc, MEng

On the Efficient Frontier (EF):

The third and the most important flaw of the EF is that it defines risk as the standard deviation of returns (volatility). This may be reasonable in a "normal" Gaussian model, but it is incongruent with what happens in real life. In distribution portfolios, the

---

[59] Jim C. Otar, *Unveiling the Retirement Myth: Advanced Retirement Planning Based on Market History* (Thornhill: Otar & Associates, 2009).

RALPH E. W. LOADER

primary risk is the sequence of returns and not the volatility of returns. What makes or breaks the outcome of a portfolio is not what happens 95% of the time in "normal" markets, but what happens in 5% of the time in "extreme" markets, up or down. Therefore, 95% of the data included in the statistical analysis corrupts its conclusions to the point of uselessness.[60]

On Monte Carlo Simulations (MC):

MC simulation is based on statistical randomness around a predefined straight line. Increasing the envelope of these outcomes does not make it more accurate. If the model does not fit well, then running one million simulations instead of one hundred does not make it any more accurate.

Some simulators add two additional, smaller distribution curves to each side of the main distribution curve. This is (supposedly) to account for the higher than "normal" occurrence of such market extremes. These are known as "fat tails." Yes, this can definitely simulate the higher occurrence of the volatility of returns at these extremes, but their random occurrence in the simulator prevents it from simulating the sequence of returns of such extremes in any realistic way.[61]

And lest you think Jim does not feel strongly about this, he goes on:

The greatest danger and impediment to the advancement of the mathematics of distribution is the fabrication of useless studies by researchers using Monte Carlo simulators. Their findings from these flawed research studies are applied to asset allocation, portfolio optimization, diversification, risk management and other aspects of retirement planning, investment management, pension management and actuarial calculations. I cringe every time I look at a publication that includes the words, 'using a Monte Carlo simulator,' 'scientific study,' 'our conclusion is...'

[60] Otar, *Unveiling the Retirement Myth*, 138.
[61] Otar, *Unveiling the Retirement Myth*, 145.

in the same article. Our money, trillions of dollars, is managed based on such flawed models and assumptions.[62]

"I see misguided fiduciaries...
... they're everywhere...
... they walk around like everyone else...
They don't even know that they are being
had by Gaussian Mindset baloney"

Gaussian Mindset Baloney

"If You Miss the Best…"

Perhaps the best chapter in Jim's book is chapter 27, "If you Miss the Best…" In it, his charming skepticism bordering on cynicism, Jim attacks the investment industry's simplistic intimidation tactics wherein the industry eschews any attempt at market timing, employing ill-considered arguments like "If you missed the best 50 days of the market, your return over the last 10 years would be -1%."[63] Why, he wonders, do they not tell you, "If you missed the worst 50 days in the last 25 years, your annual return would be +25%"[64]? The following

---

[62] Otar, *Unveiling the Retirement Myth*, 155.

[63] Otar, *Unveiling the Retirement Myth*, 285.

[64] Otar, *Unveiling the Retirement Myth*, 285.

table extracts a few rows and columns from Jim's table 27.1.[65] If you consider the numbers carefully, I think they speak for themselves; they raise the question "In light of the considerable advantage accruing to those who successfully avoid major negative tail events, should we not apply ourselves more diligently, always within a disciplined, objectives-driven risk-managed framework, to the effort of managing downside risk? Is not the opportunity cost, namely, the potential sacrifice of some measured upside market capture, a reasonable price of admission?"

In a world where objectives may be simply stated as "absolute capital preservation," the numbers decree that we should and that it is! More complex, growing liability-driven investment objectives will necessarily complicate the risk assessment exercise, but in light of the compelling numbers in the following chart, complex investment objectives alone should not negate the worthiness of the assessment exercise itself.

Effect of Missing the Best or the Worst Months[66]

Over 108 Years	Missed Best Months		Missed Worst Months	
Number of Months Missed	$1,000 invested becomes	Compound Annual Return	$1,000 invested becomes	Compound Annual Return
10	$18,680	2.70%	$1,612,958	6.94%
50	$310	-1.06%	$224,575,874	11.84%
150	$0.44	-6.77%	$201,317,127,876	18.97%

[65] Otar's preamble to the table, which explains his methodology, reads as follows: "Here is my research based on the DJIA between January 1, 1900 and December 31, 2008. I used a pure index return, no dividends, no transaction fees and no interest income while money sits in cash. We invest $1,000 at the beginning of 1900 (buy and hold). I also changed my time interval from days to months. If I am going to miss anything, it is more logical to miss months rather than days. There are 1305 months during this time period (markets were closed for some months in 1914)."

[66] Extract from Otar's table 27.1: The Effect of Missing the Best or the Worst Months—Measured Over 108.75 Years (1305 months).

Another student of risk management is Joe Nocera, whose *New York Times* article "Risk Mismanagement" addressed the pros and cons of the most popular of risk management tools, "VaR" (value at risk), at a time (January 2009) when risk managers everywhere were reeling from the onslaught of too many extreme market events, including the collapse resulting from the 2008 financial crisis. He explains,

> VaR measures the boundaries of risk in a portfolio over short durations, assuming a "normal" market…given the calamity that has since occurred, there has been a great deal of talk, even in quant circles, that this widespread institutional reliance on VaR was a terrible mistake.[67]

Nocera quotes several practitioners whose VaR experiences left them with a decidedly jaundiced view of the model's utility, but he also spoke with the people from RiskMetrics, one of the better known risk modelling firms. Importantly, Greg Berman of RiskMetrics notes, "A computer does not do risk modeling, people do it…this was much more a failure of management than it was of risk management…you can't blame math." Nocera comments, "The problem on Wall Street at the end of the housing bubble is that all judgment was cast aside," and he credits Goldman Sachs' ability to sidestep much of the fallout of the financial crisis with their recognition that "the math alone was never going to be enough."

Are there one or two key lessons about risk management that we can take away from the work of these thought leaders on the subject? I think so. First, we do need to acknowledge that risk modelling entails the use of assumptions regarding the distribution of returns (a "normal" distribution or something like it) that may be useful for longer-term planning purposes but are certainly ineffective in their ability to enable us to predict shorter-term outcomes. With that caveat in mind we should heed Bob Collie's admonition that "models should serve as an aid to understanding and not a replacement for it." We must remember to build judgment into all of our risk management processes, long-

---

[67] Joe Nocera, "Risk Mismanagement," *The New York Times* (January 4, 2009).

and short-term ones. Of course, where we open the door to judgment, dissent walks in and life gets tough; so it does, so it is.

Our second lesson arises from Jim Otar's work on the importance of the "sequence of returns." We need to know that addressing long-term risk alone is insufficient because extreme events in the near term hold the potential to seriously undermine our ability to achieve longer-term targets. This is so for two reasons—*mathematically* because of the tendency for extremely negative market events to wreck the anticipated benefit of compounding returns and *behaviourally* because of the tendency for people to react in a counterproductive way by rendering decisions based on our emotional response to extreme market events (the natural inclination to "buy high and sell low"). Hence we do need to build into our risk management system a process for recognizing that short-term risk is a reality that needs to be understood and addressed.

Today mechanisms for the responsible risk management of institutionally invested funds are available. Consistent with the lessons we have learned, we conclude that risk management necessarily takes the form of a two-pronged attack; at Level 1 risk management addresses policy (or what some prefer to label "strategic") issues with a long-term focus. (Note that I define "long-term" as concerning itself with the ultimate result, 15 to 40 years from now, of decisions taken today; the "short-term" concerns itself with what may happen at any point in time over the next 15 years and the interim and longer-term impact of such shorter-term events.) At Level 2 risk management addresses tactical issues with a focus on concerns regarding extreme short-term market events. The "average" pension fund, for example, might well address their risk management challenge today by employing "Liability Driven"[68] investment thinking to tackle Level 1 policy issues and some form of tactical asset allocation strategy to deal with Level 2 tactical

---

[68] Bob Collie, "Don't Marry a Model," *Russell Viewpoint* (Russell Investments, February 2011), notes, "A popular path through this maze is to move in stages as funded status improves, an approach known as liability-responsive asset allocation (or LRAA). It is possible to tie LRAA not only to funded status but also to the level of interest rates, and hence to build some consideration of valuation levels in to the timing of the evolution in strategy." See also Jim Gannon and Bob Collie, "Liability-Responsive Asset Allocation," *Russell Viewpoint* (Russell Investments, April 2009).

issues. Of course, there is no "average" fund. Each fund is unique, and each fund will therefore utilize suitable combinations of information and analytics, asset and liability models, investment products and overlays all subject to the unique characteristics, risk tolerances, judgmental oversight and investment beliefs and policies of the stakeholder/trustees for the institutional fund concerned.

Comprehensive risk management systems then include, but are not limited to, mathematical models. Judgment is a significant part of the risk management exercise. Given the complexity and uniqueness of each fund's profile, the required combination of products and services are not likely to be found all in one place. Furthermore, getting to the point of implementation of a carefully considered risk management program is a demanding exercise for a full-time dedicated team of investment professionals; it is all the more demanding for a diverse committee-driven structure with people from different professional backgrounds and sometimes conflicting interests.

Hard work, yes, but cutting through much of the gobbledygook, risk management is significantly common sense and good judgment. Unfortunately, when we match the volume and complexity of alternative approaches against each fund's unique characteristics, choosing the right path is difficult; shortcuts are deceptively easy but are often short on the essential ingredients—common sense and good judgment.

CHAPTER 8

Institutional Investment Roundup (GPR)

"I slept and dreamt that life was joy. I awoke and saw that life was service.
I acted and behold, service was joy."
Rabindranath Tagore

SUMMING UP TO THIS POINT, HERE IS WHAT WE HAVE LEARNED:

1. Critical skepticism rules; it is a happy state of mind.
2. Noise trading is a deadly investment disease, "meaningless, a chasing after the wind."[69]
3. We're not as smart as we think we are; we have a responsibility to be skeptical…first of ourselves.
4. Beyond skepticism, a framework for actionable decisions: governance, policy and risk management are the essential keys to a better investment world.
5. Central themes upon which to build the framework: core values and leadership—"the harvest is plentiful but the workers are few."[70]
6. Six principles for best practice pension fund governance: our two central themes (core values and leadership) plus
   a) Mission clarity
   b) A statement of investment beliefs
   c) A liability-aware risk management process
   d) Effective time and resource management

---

[69] Ecclesiastes 1:14.
[70] Matthew 9:37.

7. Leadership and core values; have I said this before?

8. The pension plan—assets, liabilities and all related agreements and policies—is one, a single entity to be managed accordingly.

9. "The essence of investment management," said legendary investor Benjamin Graham, "is the management of risks, not the management of returns."

10. If the benchmark is wrong, analytics are wrong; if analytics are wrong, conclusions are wrong and so are decisions that derive from those conclusions.

11. Never marry a model; you will never experience a "normal" market. Risk is long-term and it is short-term. Risk management is common sense (judgment) and it is hard work.

And here is what I conclude…

I noted earlier that investment policies and risk management are distinctly part of the overall governance project; they simply roll up as critical pieces of the governance puzzle. So the essential question is "What exactly do we achieve through better governance?" Governance is rules—rules for planning, organization, implementation and control; rules of engagement and rules of behavior. Governance is self-imposed rules that we believe will guide our decisions and our actions so as to yield a better outcome in relation to our highest mission. In the foregoing discussion of the thought processes and activities required to responsibly address investment governance we have a preview of the burden of associated challenges—of the sheer hard work that is part and parcel of the exercise. Do we really need to engage in this formidable undertaking? I think you know the answer; and here, based on what we have already learned, as simply as I can state it, is the supportive rationale for my argument in favour of a critically skeptical mindset and better governance:

1. We are not as smart as we think we are.

2. We are not as strong as we think we are.

3. We are not as ethical, as caring and as respectful of others as we would like to be.

So we need rules as our guide, rules that are considered and conceived in the good times so that when the bad times are upon us, as they surely will be, we will have a chance—not a certainty, but a higher probability and some hope—that we will be better prepared and smart enough, strong enough, ethical, caring and respectful enough to shoulder the worst of times in the certain knowledge that the sun will rise tomorrow as the best of times unfold once more.

CHAPTER 9

Then There Is Faith

"My own buffoonery can be real and of the most profound substance, pure humbug. I am constantly in a dilemma: I do not know when I start to pretend or when I tell the truth."
Salvador Dali

"But where can wisdom be found?
Where does understanding dwell?"
Job 28:12

"Truly I tell you, if you have faith as small as a mustard seed, you can say to this mountain, 'Move from here to there,' and it will move. Nothing will be impossible for you."
Matthew 17:20

"And if I have a faith that can move mountains,
but do not have love, I am nothing."
1 Corinthians 13:2

"Everyone who loves has been born of God and knows God. Whoever does not love does not know God, because God is love."
1 John 4:7–8

ARE RULES REALLY ENOUGH? SOUND GOVERNANCE PROVIDES A TEMPLATE, a reference point for effective organization and exemplary behavior under challenging circumstances, "grace under fire" as it were. But what assurance do we have that we will adhere to the plan, or that we are capable of doing so, since we have already acknowledged that we are not smart enough, strong enough, ethical, caring and respectful enough to do so? The stories cited in the early chapters of this book provide ample evidence that human ingenuity, our infinite capacity for rationalization, readily enables us to disregard established facts, rules or norms that don't coincide with our own world view. My own experience, and but for a matter of degree likely yours too, has taught me to be wary, skeptical of people's motivations, when stress enters the room. Too many times I have witnessed otherwise very ethical, well-intentioned people resort to devious, even hurtful behaviour in order to attain the upper hand in hard-fought negotiations. I have seen initially harmonious discussion turn to acrimony and bitterness. I have seen friends become enemies. I have seen man's best laid plans, the soundest of governance structures and painstakingly documented rules ignored, flouted, lost in a war of egos.

We are counseled as to the importance of controlling our thoughts in the following oft-used quotation:

> Sow a thought, and you reap an act;
> Sow an act, and you reap a habit;
> Sow a habit, and you reap a character;
> Sow a character and you reap a destiny.[71]

But how do we win this battle for our own destiny, this struggle with our own human nature for control over our own thoughts? How do we subdue ego in favour of the greater good? Must we remain prisoners to the limitations of our own humanity?

---

[71] Ascribed to Charles Reade, an English novelist, 1814–1884, in *Notes and Queries* (9th Series), vol. 12, October 17, 1903, though there seems some uncertainty about the quotation's original source.

Surely we must not!

And thankfully, there is an answer to this dilemma—one not based on scientific pragmatism or on the methodological skepticism espoused in earlier chapters or on sound governance, policy and risk management, GPR. Rather, our answer springs from the more qualitative, less tangible dimensions of life, on the certainty that life is defined not only by its physical and mental nature but, very importantly, by a spiritual dimension. For the most part all reference to the spiritual dimension of life eludes finite description in material or scientific terms, and therefore we seek understanding of spirituality through the study of faith.

And suddenly, our story takes on new meaning! Discussion of "faith" in a dissertation primarily concerned with money seems almost a contradiction in terms. Certainly we open the door to controversy of a very different nature than that engendered by concerns relating to the skeptical mindset and sound investment governance practices. Use of the term "faith" in business and polite social circles tends to give rise to nervous laughter. Most people prefer not to get into it, because faith is perceived as a "personal" matter, discussion of which risks offending those whom we engage in the dialogue. I disagree; surely there is room in this world for reasoned, respectful discussion and debate on all matters central to our existence and to the meaning we attach to life. In his book *What Money Can't Buy—The Moral Limits of Markets*, Michael Sandel talks, in the context of politics, to the importance of discourse that embraces moral and spiritual content:

> Our politics is overheated because it is mostly vacant, empty of moral and spiritual content. It fails to engage with big questions that people care about…In hopes of avoiding sectarian strife, we often insist that citizens leave their moral and spiritual convictions behind when they enter the public square…A debate about the moral limits of markets would enable us to decide, as a society, where markets serve the public good and where they don't belong. It would also invigorate our politics, by welcoming competing notions of the good life into the public square…It would be folly to expect that a morally more robust public discourse, even at its best, would lead to agreement on every contested question.

But it would make for a healthier public life. And it would make us more aware of the price we pay for living in a society where everything is up for sale…

What matters is that people of different backgrounds and social positions encounter one another, and bump up against one another, in the course of everyday life. For this is how we learn to negotiate and abide our differences, and how we come to care for the common good.[72]

So now we add faith to our recipe for the essential disciplines of institutional investment management, life and happiness, and we have

- ~ 2 cups governance
- ~ 3 tablespoons policy
- ~ 1 full measure of risk management kneaded carefully throughout
- ~ Then baked forever at body temperature in an oven called faith!

And our final ingredient must be justified. Nothing short of full transparency will suffice. We need a clear definition of the meaning that we ascribe to the term "faith," and in the context of this text we must explain just how faith can work to give us victory in the battle over our own human nature. I have heard it said that the writing of one book gives birth to ideas that inevitably lead to the writing of another book. There can be no doubt that the subject of "faith" justifies a book of its own—one that I may get to some day. But for our purposes here I feel it best to strive for simplicity, for a certain economy of words, in order to make my point clearly and concisely. This entails considerable risk, of course, since the "faith" to which I refer is distinctly a faith in God, and "the relationship between God and humanity has never been simple."[73] But institutional investors are accustomed to dealing with risk and so will appreciate and understand my willingness to do so here. It should also be said here that

---

[72] Michael J. Sandel, *What Money Can't Buy: The Moral Limits of Markets* (New York: Farrar, Strauss and Giroux, 2012), 13-14, 203.

[73] Jeff Veenstra, "The Gospel Summarized: Show God's Kindness to Others," *Presbyterian Record* (December 2012), 8. Rev. Veenstra is the minister at The Church of St. Andrew and St. Paul, Montreal.

in this chapter I have allowed myself some discretion (arguably too much discretion) in revealing the doctrines that I have embraced in my own personal faith. I have done so for purposes of transparency, for clarity in establishing the flow of logic, and so that you may consider whether this faith that has been so helpful in my own life may also work for you.

To adequately convey my understanding of faith and its role in relation to investing, life and happiness, the remainder of this book tackles a few key theological issues head on, defining certain doctrines for clarity's sake and concluding with a simple explanation of how faith has made a difference to my personal investment philosophy and to the way in which I live and enjoy my life. The doctrines on which I have chosen to elaborate are necessarily Christian doctrines, since my roots and my learning have been based in Christianity, but readers are free to apply their own cultural and religious grounding in an attempt to link their chosen faith to the conclusions that I draw for investing, life and happiness. Before I launch us into our discussion of theology and doctrine however, and particularly for those not inclined to go there, here are three sentences that attempt to capture the rationale that I offer for the importance of faith to your investment choices, to quality and purpose in your life and ultimately to your personal happiness.

I have employed the term "faith" inasmuch as it requires of us an unloading of the baggage of ego-driven perceptions, the hubris that we have accumulated through years of life experience. In a word, faith maintains the centrality of a single human value, humility—humility in the sense of forgoing personal credit for victory and blame for defeat, and admitting that we ourselves are not in control but that there is, in fact, a greater power, a loving and caring power, in control. Paradoxically, it is this humble admission that frees us to embrace the confident knowledge that while it may be true that we alone are not smart enough, strong enough, ethical, caring and respectful enough to stay the course and win the day, "with God all things are possible."[74]

---

[74] Matthew 19:26: "Jesus looked at them and said, 'With man this is impossible, but with God all things are possible.'"

RALPH E. W. LOADER

Defining Faith

So what is "faith"? I fear that today's increasingly secular world has lost interest in the very idea of faith. For many people, the word "faith" evokes ideas of conformist ideology—hoards of mindless sheep acting out their daily lives based upon a set of unfounded, unexamined and unchanging beliefs that are promulgated by an oligopoly of religious institutions bent on self-preservation and aggrandizement. If that is faith, it is no wonder that the world has lost interest and considers further discussion fruitless. But that is not faith at all! There is a word, though, to describe that particular perception of faith. The word is "fideism," which is "the name given to that school of thought which (argues) that faith is in some sense independent of, if not outright adversarial toward, reason."[75] In his book *Faith Seeking Understanding*, Daniel Migliore notes, "True faith must be distinguished from fideism. Fideism says there comes a point where we must stop asking questions and must simply believe; faith keeps on seeking and asking."[76] This is surely a crucial distinction for anyone curious about the nature and reason for being, the meaning and purpose of life, in particular their own. That should include all of us, although some days I really do wonder about that notion. The idea that faith "keeps on seeking and asking" lends credibility to the concept that is the antithesis of conformist dogma. Faith, in Migliore's context, assumes the character of a perpetual and robust research effort rooted in, rather than opposed to reason. Like success, faith is "a journey, not a destination," and if more people were to understand it this way we would likely experience a much broader and more active engagement in the discussion.

Of course, every journey does have an intended destination, and every journey travels a route that one believes offers a reasonable likelihood of reaching one's intended destination. Here the discussion gets a little more challenging. If faith is our journey, what is our intended destination, i.e., our purpose or objective? And what route (belief set) have we chosen to get there? In this regard people will

---

[75] *Stanford Encyclopedia of Philosophy*, s.v. "Fideism."
[76] Daniel L. Migliore, *Faith Seeking Understanding* (Grand Rapids: Wm. B. Eerdmans Publishing Co., 2004), 3.

differ, but it is indisputable that we are all on the journey; we are all people of faith.

The question of the route (belief set) is addressed further on, but in any business, the investment business or the business of life, our first item of discussion is always our objectives. First we set our objectives and then we go about figuring out how we are going to achieve them. On our journey of faith we are all free to choose our own objectives, our own destination, but despite the uniqueness of our individual intended destinations, ultimately our destinations all converge towards a single place and time that we call "truth." We are on this journey to uncover the truth about all things—something we have shown in earlier chapters that none of us, not even the very best and brightest of us, possesses. Why, we can't even solve the problems of a global financial system or of the global economy! How can we expect to come to grips with the complexities surrounding and permeating the nature and reason for being, the meaning and purpose of life? So our journey of faith has as its destination a single objective: truth.

Recall that in chapter 1 I spoke of the importance of skepticism, specifically "methodological skepticism," which, as an approach to thought, subjects all knowledge claims to scrutiny with the goal of sorting out true from false claims. To reiterate, "sorting out true from false—there it is; more true, more happy." If truth is directly proportional to happiness, the search for truth is surely a worthy objective. But before we set out in search of truth, we will be wise to undertake a little research into the state of the roads along the route that we choose to travel. For if the roads that we travel are paved only with good intentions, we risk serious mishap; we must ensure that healthy skepticism is woven into each mile of our roadbed construction material. For absent skepticism as our constant travel companion we are the willing target of those who would wrongly brand our journey "fideism" or "conformist dogma." On this journey we reject fideism; we reject dogma. This is a journey of faith, the definition of which we can now clearly state as "a quest for truth rooted in, rather than opposed to, reason." Importantly, in Migliore's words our quest "keeps on seeking and asking"; it is characterized by an attitude of humility and resolve, never hubris.

97

Still, in today's productivity oriented, multi-tasking societies, people for the most part have little time or inclination to think about, let alone to study and understand, the history and evolution of theological thought. And we must be fair in acknowledging that church history has had a hand in shaping the world's perception of faith and the general disinclination to seek any further understanding. Indeed church history, i.e., the history of churches of all faiths, is littered with periods when dogmatic constructs were espoused and resulting behaviour was poor at best, disastrous at worst. Disenchanted by this observed behaviour, society in good measure has turned a deaf ear, no longer willing to engage in the debate over faith. In the process people have failed to notice how, with lessons learned, change has asserted itself on the church, how over several decades now, leading thinkers in the world's theological community have re-opened the dialogue in a continuing quest for truth, rooted in reason.

Rooted in reason as it is, this journey of faith must originate in a reasoned belief set; we must travel a road that we believe will lead to our ultimate destination—truth. In scientific terms, we need a hypothesis that our journey will serve to prove or to disprove. And we embark on this journey, traveling this road courageously in the full knowledge that we will not reach our destination in our lifetime on this earth. I noted earlier on that I have defined my hypothesis, I have chosen my road; its name is "Christian faith." Like any road not yet traveled, this road is a quest; it is a personal, perpetual and robust research effort, a search for truth rooted in reason. So come, travel this road with me for just a little while longer; together let's see what myths we may dispel, what truths we may uncover.

What Do Christians Believe?

To answer this question we now engage in the realm of theology, specifically the discipline called "systematic theological reflection." The Greek translation of the word "theology" is "the study of God," and the central purpose of systematic theology is to understand more about (or to draw nearer to) God. For purposes of this book, "systematic theological reflection" becomes "Christian systematic theology," which is my quest for truth. employing the working hypothesis that the source of all truth is the Christian God. Proverbs 1:7 states, "The fear of the Lord is the beginning of knowledge." Further, the limitations of humanity render faith indispensable to any understanding of God. As Isaiah 55:8–9 teaches, "'For my thoughts are not your thoughts, neither are your ways my ways,' declares the Lord. 'As the heavens are higher than the earth, so are my ways higher than your ways and my thoughts than your thoughts.'" If our working hypothesis holds true, that the Christian God is the source of all truth, or, stated more strongly, God is truth, then this understanding of the purpose of our journey and the road we have chosen is clear, simple and profound.

Indeed, the objects of theological study are noble ones. Migliore[77] and Grenz,[78] whose texts I rely upon heavily for this discussion, and Pannenberg[79] cite numerous reasons in support of the study of theology as a discipline. Summarizing selectively I offer the following list of six:

1. the articulation of the Christian faith,
2. understanding…of God, truth and the meaning of life,
3. the unearthing of joy and happiness,
4. instruction towards wisdom and judgment,
5. self-identity within a community and
6. resolution of the problem of theodicy, i.e., to explain how the existence of evil in the world can be reconciled with the justice and goodness of God.

If my modest effort at theological expression achieves any of these worthy objectives with even a few readers of this script, my purpose in the writing will be accomplished. I should be clear, though, that my purpose is less the articulation of the Christian faith than it is the articulation of *my* Christian faith. I emphasize "my" Christian faith because it would be presumptuous and misleading of me to suggest that I can correctly articulate "the" Christian faith for all believers or, for that

---

[77] Migliore, *Faith Seeking Understanding.*

[78] Stanley J. Grenz, *Theology for the Community of God* (Grand Rapids: Wm. B. Eerdmans Publishing Co., 2000).

[79] Wolfhart Pannenberg, *An Introduction to Systematic Theology* (Grand Rapids: Wm. B. Eerdmans Publishing Co., 1991).

matter, for anyone but myself. As it is true that through the centuries the world's most respected Christian theologians have themselves developed different views in respect of important Christian doctrines, I, a lay person within the Christian community, can lay claim only to an attempt to outline critical elements of my own faith as it has grown out of my personal experience, study and deliberation. But please don't let the uncertainty of it all scare you off. In the mystery is the beauty, and a lengthy dissertation is not my intention—quite the contrary. As already mentioned, clarity and brevity are my intention—simplicity, with all the risk that it entails. In fact, the paragraphs that follow speak briefly to five central Christian doctrines that I have decided should be sufficient in all to make the points with which this text is concerned. The doctrines that I attend to here address the following questions:

- Who is this God that Christians espouse? (The doctrine of God and the Trinity)
- Is the Bible true? (The authority of Scripture)
- Why do bad things happen to good people? (Providence and evil—the problem of theodicy)
- How do Christians relate to other religions? (Religious pluralism)
- Why should I go to church? ("Community" as God's purpose)

The Doctrine of God and the Trinity

In his *The Summa Theologica* (article 7), St. Thomas Aquinas asks, "Is God the subject of this science (the science of theology)?"[80] And he concludes, in part, "Though we cannot know what God is, nevertheless this teaching employs an effect of his, of nature or of grace, in place of a definition, and by this means discusses truths about him." So let's begin by agreeing with Aquinas that "we cannot know what God is" and yet with a determination nonetheless to seek what knowledge we can in light of the very worthy objectives that theological study holds out for us.

Efforts to articulate a doctrine of God seem to begin with an undertaking to "characterize" God by using all available information to establish what we understand to be the "attributes of God." There are numerous attributes that various theologians ascribe to the Christian

---

[80] St. Thomas Aquinas, *The Summa Theologica* (Westminster: Christian Classics, 1981).

God. These include some of the better known attributes, such as "omniscience" (knows everything), "omnipotence" (all-powerful), "eternal" (not confined to time), "holy" (perfect), "just" (fair in all His actions) and "loving" (exhibits a love not based on the worth or merit of the object of His love), and many other lesser known attributes as well. What, though, do we believe are the most important claims about our God? According to Cobb and Griffin (i.e., the "process" school of theology):

1. By definition the divine reality is perfect
2. The basic character of this divine reality is best described by the term "love."[81]

In some senses, the claim of perfection may be in itself a sufficient descriptor for God, since we can maintain that He is perfect in respect of all attributes, including love. Nevertheless, according to Cobb and Griffin the traditional theology school argues that, to the extent that love is *both* creative and compassionate, a contradiction arises, since compassion necessitates adjustment by God in order to act compassionately in response to human circumstances. And adjustment implies change from the divine that is perfect to a divine that is something other than perfect.

At this point, allow me a momentary digression. The study of theology is full of such questions: Is God perfect, or is He compassionate, or is He both? You may feel, as I often do, that this sort of discussion is as meaningful as the question "How many angels can you fit on the head of a pin?" After all, knowledge is not faith (which is belief), and faith is not knowledge. So why expend all that energy striving for knowledge of things that are most likely not fully knowable? Thinking this question through a little, I guess it would be fair to say that the greater the knowledge (and therefore the understanding) that supports your faith, the greater the likelihood that you will act on that faith. And since it is important not only to have faith but also to act upon it (this, by the way, is another point of contention for our most learned

---

[81] John B. Jr. Cobb and David Ray Griffin, *Process Theology: An Introductory Exposition* (Westminster: The Westminster Press, 1976), 44.

theologians), we should now return to the question of whether God is perfect, compassionate or both. In answer to the question, Cobb and Griffin argue,

> While perfection entails independence or absoluteness in some respects, it also entails dependence or relativity in other respects. It entails ethical independence…(but) to promote the greatest good, one must be informed by, and thus relativized by, the feelings of others.[82]

I want my God to be both perfect (holy) and compassionate (love), but I also want a better understanding of just how this could be so. Despite the apparent contradiction between these two attributes, Trinitarian doctrine holds the key to an understanding of how the God of the Christian narrative can be both holy and love, just as God the Trinity is three and God is one.

Trinitarian Doctrine

Although we find no specific mention of the Trinity in the Bible, ideas regarding the existence of a triune God emerge quite naturally from the days of the apostles as they experienced life on earth with Jesus and with the Holy Spirit. Before we address the meaning of our belief in the triune God, some historical context will serve to distinguish our understanding of the particular nature and characteristics of this triune God.

The reality of the risen Christ posed a dilemma for the early disciples. "Their faith required that they bring together three different strands of belief: the heritage of monotheism, the confession of Jesus' lordship and the experience of the presence of the Holy Spirit."[83] Four centuries of creative thinking brought us to the current formulation, simply (but arguably incomprehensibly) stated as "one essence, three persons."

The question of just how the three comprise the one God, i.e., the relationship of Father, Son and Spirit, was tackled by the Cappadocian

---

[82] Cobb and Griffin, *Process Theology*, 46, 47.

[83] Grenz, *Theology for the Community of God*, 54.

fathers—Basil, Gregory of Nyssa and Gregory of Nazianzus, who declared that God is one *ousia* (essence) and three *hypostatseis* (independent realities) that share the same will, nature and essence. The Trinitarian distinctions, Father, Son and Holy Spirit, belong to the eternal nature of God.[84] I borrow further on Grenz in this paraphrased attempt to project a visualization of the differentiation of Father, Son and Holy Spirit:

Each of the three Trinitarian members fulfills a specific role in the one divine program. The Father functions as the ground of the world and of the divine program for creation. The Son functions as the revealer of God, the exemplar and herald of the Father's will for creation, and the redeemer of humankind. And the Spirit functions as the personal divine power active in the world, the completer of the divine will and program… despite their varying functions in the one divine program, all are involved in every area of God's working in the world (in creation, in reconciliation and in the completion of the divine program)…and the economic unity of the Trinitarian members also means that each is dependent on the work of the others for the fulfillment of the one divine program.

The New Testament (specifically, 1 John 4:7–21) suggests that the ontological (def: "Of or relating to the argument for the existence of God") unity which the three constitute and therefore which comprises the divine essence is agape (love)…the assertion that love forms the foundation of the unity in the one God opens a window on the divine reality. The unity of God is nothing less than the self dedication of the Trinitarian persons to each other. Indeed, God is love—the divine essence is the love that binds together the Trinity. As the apostolic writer indicates, the essence of God is love. The doctrine of the Trinity indicates how this is the case.

---

[84] Taken from Grenz, *Theology for the Community of God*, 60–61.

Grenz goes on to say that

- the essence of God is love,
- love is the fundamental attribute of God and
- love is the fundamental characteristic of God in relationship with creation.[85]

So I contend that

a) God is three independent realities in unity, each fulfilling a specific role in the one divine program, and

b) God is love, free of constraints, internal to the Trinity and flowing outwardly by grace into creation.

But what does all this mean to me and to you? I will try to answer this question, under three broad headings.

Christian Ethics, Christian Values

In the first instance, per Migliore,

> The Christian understanding of human life and Christian social ethics are grounded in Trinitarian theology…the Christian hope for peace with justice and freedom in community among peoples of diverse cultures, races, and gender corresponds to the Trinitarian logic of God.[86]

Migliore speaks of relationships defined by honour and respect among equals as having its basis in the divine way of life.

Grenz elaborates as follows:

1. In His eternal essence the one God is a social reality, the social Trinity.
2. The ethical life, therefore, is the life-in-relationship, or the life-in-community.
3. Love stands as the ideal and the standard for human life as well:

---

[85] Taken from Grenz, *Theology for the Community of God*, 66–69 and 71–72.
[86] Migliore, *Faith Seeking Understanding*, 80.

a) Our task is to seek to reflect God's loving concern for all creatures in our natural environment.

b) God loves each human being and therefore He demands that we act justly.

c) We must see the entire world as the object of our care and concern.[87]

Meaning and Hope

Secondly, for purposes of education and apologetics towards meaning and hope for all creation, "The doctrine of the Trinity is the church's effort to give coherent expression to this mystery of God's grace announced in the gospel and experienced in Christian faith."[88] If we are cognizant of the limitations of humanity (and of all creation), if we hunger for the truth and hope for a renewed world of peace and justice for all, for "victory of divine love over all evil and the participation of creation in God's eternal joy,"[89] the triune God, and only the triune God, is of the essence, the attributes and the activity to deliver. That is to say, only the triune God can impart meaning to our lives. "As John Calvin insisted, our knowledge of God and our knowledge of ourselves are always inextricably intertwined."[90]

Thinking of the Trinity in retrospect, in the here and now, and prospectively, "looking ahead to the glorious completion of the purpose for which God created and reconciled the world…declares that all of the works of God—creation, reconciliation, and redemption—have their beginning and goal in the free grace of God made known supremely in Jesus Christ. It affirms that the triune God who lives eternally in communion graciously wills to include others in that communion."[91]

We can also enjoy renewed meaning and power in our prayer life as we grow in our understanding of the nature of the triune God who calls us to pray and who responds to prayer. Cognizance of the doctrine

---

[87] Paraphrased from Grenz, 74–76.

[88] Migliore, *Faith Seeking Understanding*, 67.

[89] Migliore, *Faith Seeking Understanding*, 133.

[90] Migliore, *Faith Seeking Understanding*, 64 quoting Calvin, *Institutes of the Christian Religion*, 1.1.1.

[91] Migliore, *Faith Seeking Understanding*, 82, 88–89.

of the Trinity will facilitate a consciousness of whom we address in prayer.[92]

Power, Love, Community

And finally, our understanding of the triune God contributes to our understanding of God's omnipotence within the world and its significance for us, individually and in community with all of creation. As Migliore says,

> A revolution in our understanding of the true power of God and of fruitful human power is implied when God is described as triune. God is *not* absolute power, *not* infinite egocentrism, *not* majestic solitariness. The power of the triune God is not coercive but creative, sacrificial and empowering love; and the glory of the triune God consists not in dominating others but in sharing life with others…To confess that God is triune is to affirm that the eternal life of God is personal life in relationship…defined (Barth and Rahner) by intersubjectivity, shared consciousness, faithful relationships, and the mutual giving and receiving of love…To confess that God is triune is to affirm that the life of God is essentially self-giving love whose strength embraces vulnerability…(that) there is no salvation for the creature apart from sharing in God's agapic (loving) way of life in solidarity and hope for the whole creation (cf. Rom. 8:18–39).[93]

It is evident from the historical review set out at the beginning of this section on Trinitarian doctrine that our thinking about God is very much a struggle in a journey whose end we will not see until the day the Lord returns. Within the Christian community itself, debate on certain details rages on. Hence the understanding of the triune God that I have used to expand on the *meaning* of my belief system is less an "answer" than it is a studied, transparent and intellectually honest "response" to the question "Who is your Christian God?" It is a carefully considered position, a belief in which I have chosen to root my world view and

---

[92] Grenz, *Theology for the Community of God*, 74–75.
[93] Migliore, *Faith Seeking Understanding*, 72, 76-77, 81.

shape my thoughts and actions in response to my experience within the world. But it will not go unchallenged. Contemplation of the many as yet unresolved details makes plain that alternatives to the precise expression of the triune God, as understood and presently applied in the Western Church, are conceivable. Any such expressions, of course, would likely be less consistent with our other contemporary doctrines, and the whole system would have to be rethought—discomforting, but a possibility for which systematic theologians are prepared should the occasion arise, for "now we see but a poor reflection as in a mirror; then we shall see face to face. Now I know in part; then I shall know fully, even as I am fully known. And now these three remain: faith, hope and love. But the greatest of these is love" (1 Corinthians 13:12–13). So it is clear that the revelation of God is not finished; the narrative unfolds and

> The truth is that neither "Scripture alone" nor "Scripture plus Church tradition" is sufficient to communicate the gospel of Christ effectively. Only the Spirit of God…is able to create and nurture faith in and obedience to Christ as Savior and Lord.[94]

The Authority of Scripture

In discourse relating to religion or specifically to Christianity, issues pertaining to the authority of Scripture are raised continually. They often take the form of questions like "Do you believe everything written in the Bible to be true?" and "How could a loving God have condoned the violence portrayed in stories of the Old Testament?" A faith whose doctrines are consistent one to another cannot escape these questions. So in this section I relate a contemporary Christian perspective on the authority of Scripture, and since I cannot do better than Migliore does in chapter 3 of his text *Faith Seeking Understanding*, this section quotes selectively but liberally from Migliore to do so. Migliore's chapter 3 begins as follows:

> Since the beginning of the church, every Christian theology has implicitly or explicitly acknowledged the authority of Scripture. The serious question has never been whether Scripture is a

---

[94] Migliore, *Faith Seeking Understanding*, 41.

primary authority for Christian faith and life, but what sort of authority it is.

For the sixteenth-century Reformers, the authority of Scripture was rooted in its liberating message, in the good news of God's gracious acceptance of sinners offered in Jesus Christ. The Bible was experienced not as an arbitrary or despotic authority but as a source of renewal, freedom and joy.

This is not the way everyone, or even every Christian, understands the meaning of scriptural authority today. Many people inside and outside the church equate the idea of the authority of the Bible with coercion rather than liberty, with terror rather than joy. They know all too well how the authority of the Bible has been invoked to suppress free inquiry and to legitimize such practices as slavery and patriarchy...I (however) contend that the authority of Scripture has to be understood in relation to its central content and its particular function within the community of faith...(for) Jesus (Himself) refused to ascribe ultimacy either to religious doctrines and traditions (Matthew 5:21; Mark 11:28) or to the claims of the state (Mark 12:13–17).

Thus, while Christian theology takes issue with the Enlightenment assumption that the only true authority is that of the independent and isolated self (an assumption also under attack by postmodern philosophy), it nevertheless engages in its own critique of oppressive authority, including versions of such authority that appear in some doctrines of Scripture. In the God of the gospel attested in Scripture, Christian faith finds the authority of liberating love that creates new community rather than an authority that works by coercive power. The gracious reign of God manifest in Jesus Christ is characterized not by authoritarian rule but by the "authoring" of new life in Christ and the new freedom for which Christ has set us free.[95]

Through the remainder of chapter 3, Migliore describes various approaches to the authority of Scripture and sets out the supportive

[95] Migliore, *Faith Seeking Understanding*, chapter 3.

rationale as well as the inadequacies of each. He then speaks to the indispensability of Scripture to our lives and to the principles of interpretation of Scripture, drawing the following important conclusions with which, in my personal faith, I concur:

- Christians do not believe in the Bible; they believe in the living God attested by the Bible.
- The Bible is the Word of God only in a derivative sense. The living Word of God is Jesus Christ.
- Scripture is thus authoritative not in itself but, as the Reformers insisted, as it 'sets forth Christ.'
- The liberation of the individual from the egocentrism, isolation, apathy and hopelessness of existence in bondage to sin and death is of fundamental importance.
- Scripture announces the beginning of a new world, new relationships, new politics in which justice prevails over injustice, friendship over hostility, mutual service over domination of some by others, and life over death.
- The faith of the church does not stand or fall with the accuracy of every detail of the gospel story, as Calvin noted,[96] but faith does stand or fall with the truthfulness of the gospel portrayal of the central events of the ministry, death, and resurrection of Christ. It matters to faith whether Jesus really befriended sinners, blessed the poor and gave his life willingly for others.
- The point is to acknowledge that Jesus Christ is alive, that we have not yet exhausted the riches of the gospel, that the Spirit brings forth new light from the Word of God, and that we are called to faithful discipleship here and now.[97]

---

[96] See John Calvin, *Commentary on a Harmony of the Evangelists*, vol. 2 (Grand Rapids; Eerdmans, 1956), 89. Cited by William C, Placher, "Contemporary Confession and Biblical Authority" in *To Confess the Faith Today*, ed. Jack L. Stotts and Jane Dempsey Douglass (Louisville: Westminster/John Knox, 1990), 71.

[97] Taken from Migliore, *Faith Seeking Understanding*, chapter 3.

And so ends our discussion of the authority of Scripture. Following on our review of the doctrine of God it should now be apparent that contemporary theology ("teaching about God") is remarkably different than that which is generally understood by much of society today, whether by people inside or outside of the church. In direct opposition to the ideas embodied in fideism and conformist dogma, today's theologians are very clearly engaged in a quest for truth rooted in reason. But to reinforce this idea, let's consider two more issues and their related Christian doctrines. First, the question of why bad things happen to good people...indeed, why evil exists at all in a world created by a just and loving God.

Providence and Evil—The Problem of Theodicy

Of the doctrinal issues confronting Christians today, the problem of theodicy is perhaps the most difficult. Theodicy is the theological discipline that seeks to explain how the existence of evil in the world can be reconciled with the justice and goodness of a providential (almighty and ever-present, all-powerful) God. Needless to say, those who would place their hope in a holy and loving God will seek resolution of this apparent contradiction, likely more so today in the wake of the horrors of two world wars and numerous other brutal social injustices witnessed through the 20th century and now witnessed daily in real time thanks to the revolution in media technology that has taken place in our own generation.

Again reaffirming the humility with which contemporary theology engages in these doctrinal challenges, Migliore opens his chapter "The Providence of God and the Mystery of Evil" with the following acknowledgment:

> Just as the condition of faith is that of seeing only dimly (1 Corinthians 13:12), so all theology is necessarily "broken thought," as Karl Barth described it. This fact comes home to us nowhere more forcefully than when we affirm the providence of God in the face of the reality of radical evil in the world. In relation to the divine providence and the "problem of evil," the

efforts of theology to clarify the claims of faith seem pitifully weak and unsatisfying.[98]

Yet reading on in Migliore, chapter 6, and with the benefit of the work of Richard Bauckham, a picture emerges of a holy God, a loving God *and* a suffering God who shares in our personal suffering and who strengthens us and emboldens us in the fight against the reality of evil in this world.[99] In the paragraphs that follow I quote selectively from these two authors in my effort to communicate more about the God in whom I believe and the theological construct that I accept in response to the question of why bad things happen to good people. My abridged version of these texts can hardly do justice to the fullness with which Migliore and Bauckham treat this crucial issue, and so I subject myself to the risks discussed earlier—risks of incompleteness, incomprehensibility and error. Duly noted, let's get on with it!

Though our authors define two kinds of evil—natural evil, "the suffering and evil that human beings experience at the hands of nature (e.g., that) caused by diseases, accidents, earthquakes, fires and floods," and moral evil, "the suffering and evil that sinful human beings inflict on each other and on the world they inhabit"—the problem of theodicy applies equally to both. Citing examples of the reality and the power of moral evil, Migliore offers,

The event of the Holocaust is particular and unique, yet the witness to what happened there is joined by witness of innocent sufferers everywhere: the black slaves in the United States, the victims of South African apartheid, the prisoners in the Stalin concentration camps, the hundreds of thousands incinerated at Hiroshima and Nagasaki, the countless number of lives lost in the Cambodian killing fields, the victims of "ethnic cleansing" in the Balkans, the millions of Rwandans slaughtered in tribal

---

[98] Migliore, *Faith Seeking Understanding*, 117.

[99] Richard Bauckham, *The Theology of Jürgen Moltmann* (Edinburgh, T&T Clark, 2006), 71–98. Jürgen Moltmann (born 8 April 1926) is a German Reformed theologian. He is a major figure in modern theology and the recipient of the 2000 Grawemeyer Award in Religion.

conflicts, the victims of "collateral damage" in various military ventures. The list is endless.[100]

And today as I write we are witness to daily reports of tragic humanitarian crises in Syria and in Mali.

Traditional theodicy arguments are several; two of the more interesting positions are noted next as extracted from *Faith Seeking Understanding*:

- Augustine: "Tyranny, injustice, social breakdown, war and other evil events are not caused by God but have their origins in the creatures' misuse of their freedom. Nevertheless, God permits these events to occur and uses them to accomplish the divine purpose. God exercises sovereignty over evil by bringing good out of what by itself is only negative and destructive."

- Those which underscore the incomprehensibility of God: "We do not know why there is so much evil in the world, or why it is distributed so unevenly, but we are nevertheless to trust God and have patience. This is a response to evil with considerable Biblical support."[101]

Both of these responses are passive in nature and understandably will be challenged as fatalist and impractical for the absence of any meaningful solutions to evil and suffering. Migliore meets these challenges later in his chapter, but I think Bauckham does so more effectively by reference to literature and to storytelling. The remainder, then, of this section on providence and evil is quoted and paraphrased from Bauckham,[102] whose chapter 4 first considers the works of three writers, Dostoyevsky, Camus and Wiesel, and pulls the strands together with thoughts drawn from the works of Moltmann.

Dostoyevsky

The first two texts, Dostoyevsky and Camus, provide a fascinating interplay that has "attained virtually scriptural status in modern

---

[100] Migliore, *Faith Seeking Understanding*, 121.

[101] Migliore, *Faith Seeking Understanding*, 122–123.

[102] Bauckham, *The Theology of Jürgen Moltmann*, 71–98.

discussions of theology." In Dostoyevsky's *The Brothers Karamazov*, Ivan Karamazov sets out his famous argument against theodicy in discussion with his brother Alyosha. His argument is against any ("final days, divine purpose") theodicy of the kind that justifies suffering as the price to be paid for the achievement of some divine purpose of God in the future.

Ivan begins,

> Listen: if all have to suffer so as to buy eternal harmony by their suffering, what have the children to do with it...? It is entirely incomprehensible why they, too, should have to suffer and why they should have to buy harmony by their sufferings. Why should they, too, be used as dung for someone's future harmony?[103]

The real force of the argument comes in this question to Alyosha:

> Tell me frankly...imagine that it is you yourself who are erecting the edifice of human destiny with the aim of making men happy in the end, of giving them peace and contentment at last, but that to do it, it is absolutely necessary, and indeed quite inevitable, to torture to death only one tiny creature, the little girl who beat her breast with her little fist, and to found the edifice on her unavenged tears—would you consent to be the architect on those conditions?[104]

"Alyosha would not. Thus the effect of the argument is that the facts of innocent and senseless suffering ought to make theodicy, in the usual sense, impossible."[105]

Camus

For Camus, the problem of the modern age...is that it began, in effect, with Ivan's principled revolt against the injustice of the

---

[103] F. Dostoevsky, *The Brothers Karamazov* (Harmondsworth: Penguin, 1982), 284.

[104] Dostoevsky, *The Brothers Karamazov*, 287.

[105] Bauckham, *The Theology of Jürgen Moltmann*, 74.

world and therefore against the God who sanctions this injustice, but it ends (for Camus writing in 1951) with the unprecedented injustices of Nazism and Stalinism...how did a movement—the modern rebellion against God—which began by rejecting the God who justifies innocent suffering end by *itself justifying* the infliction of innocent suffering on an unprecedented scale?...As Camus sees it...theodicy has been replaced by anthropodicy (an attempt, or argument attempting, to justify the existence of humanity as good)...the God of theodicy had to be rejected in the modern revolt against the injustices of his world. But the rebel who wishes to replace that world by a new just world must himself replace God. Humanity—or at least the political élite, who know there is no God—must take control of human destiny in order to replace the unjust world of the dead God with its own new world of human justice. But in order to subject history to this purpose, the revolutionary élite justifies any means...(justifies tyranny and innocent suffering for the sake of future justice). Thus, Camus's interpretation...makes clear that Ivan's atheism is not in itself a solution to the problem of theodicy because it simply gives rise to another form of the problem; that of anthropodicy.[106]

Wiesel

Elie Wiesel is a Jewish holocaust survivor and novelist whose book *La Nuit (Night)* is an autobiographical memoir of his experience of Auschwitz. The following is taken directly from Wiesel's story. For brevity's sake I have chosen to omit the bulk of Bauckham's expansion and explanation, moving instead directly to Bauckham's conclusions and Moltmann's approach to theodicy. ***A note of caution for the sensitive reader: Wiesel's story includes violence and brutality that are likely to prove extremely disturbing.***

The story takes place in Buna, the camp attached to Auschwitz. A young Jewish boy was hanged, along with two adults, by the SS in front of thousands of inmates of the camp, who were then

---

[106] Bauckham, *The Theology of Jürgen Moltmann*, 75-76.

obliged to file past the three hanged bodies, looking them full in the face. The two adults were dead, but the child, being so light, was still alive.

For more than half an hour he stayed there, struggling between life and death, dying in slow agony under our eyes. And we had to look him full in the face. He was still alive when I passed in front of him. His tongue was still red, his eyes were not yet glazed.

Behind me, I heard (a) man asking:

"Where is God now?"

And I heard a voice within me answer him:

"Where is He? Here He is—He is hanging here on this gallows..."

That night the soup tasted of corpses.[107]

Bauckham steers us away from analogies relating to the *crucified* God towards the idea that the young man's death marked Wiesel's loss of faith in God. He then concludes from the three texts that an adequate theological response to the problem of suffering must meet two requirements:

1. Innocent and involuntary suffering must not be justified. It must be justified neither by theodicy, which explains it as necessary to God's purpose, nor by anthropodicy, which explains it as necessary to some higher human purpose. Such justifications suppress the sense of moral outrage against evil, silence protest against it, and therefore at the very least reduce the motive for relieving and overcoming suffering. At worst they justify infliction of innocent suffering by totalitarian regimes both theocratic and atheistic.

2. An adequate theological response to the problem of suffering must contain an initiative for overcoming suffering. If it is not to justify suffering, it must, on the contrary, help to maintain the protest against suffering and convert it into an initiative for

---

[107] Bauckham, *The Theology of Jürgen Moltmann*, 77. Quoted text from Elie Wiesel, *Night* (New York: Hill & Wang, 1960), 71.

overcoming suffering. These two requirements are presupposed in Moltmann's approach to theodicy.[108]

Moltmann

Jürgen Moltmann's approach to theodicy is supported by his particular interpretation of the crucifixion and the resurrection together. For Moltmann the resurrection is interpreted by the concepts of divine *promise* and *hope*. The crucifixion is interpreted by the concepts of *divine suffering* and *love*.

> The contradiction of cross and resurrection corresponds to the contradiction between what reality is now and what God promises to make it…the promise sets believers in contradiction to the state of the world in which they live…and leads to attempts to transcend the contradiction as Christians seek possibilities of bringing reality into closer correspondence to the promise.
>
> As a response to the problem of suffering, therefore, Moltmann is proposing a ("final days, divine purpose") theodicy, *not* in the sense that suffering will prove justified as contributing to the final fulfilment of God's purpose, but in the sense that God will finally *overcome* all suffering…God's promise gives strength to the protest and converts it into action…but we are left wondering how a God who responds to the unjustified suffering of the world *only* with promises can ever justify himself, even when he fulfills the promises…How does the promise of liberation from suffering in God's presence, given in the resurrection, reach those who in their meaningless suffering feel abandoned by God?
>
> Moltmann's answer is that it reaches them through Jesus' *identification* with them, in their condition, on the cross…this identification involves above all a *sharing* of their suffering. It is love which willingly, out of love, comes alongside those it loves and identifies with them in their suffering (not sanctioning their suffering but purposing their liberation from it).[109]

---

[108] Bauckham, *The Theology of Jürgen Moltmann*, 81–82.

[109] Bauckham, *The Theology of Jürgen Moltmann*, 83–86.

And finally we return, for our conclusion and the required nod to humility, to Migliore, who notes,

> As Paul Helm writes, "Belief in providence enables Christians to put their pain in a different setting."...Events of horrendous evil have the capacity to shake faith to the foundations...In a world where the cycle of violence and counter-violence threatens to spin out of control, can God have a providential plan for me, for my family, for my nation, for the world? The anguish of this question cannot be removed by well-crafted theoretical theodicies.[110]

Religious Pluralism

The question of religious pluralism dogged me for decades...that is until I completed my first (and only) postgraduate course in Christian theology and discovered the very thoughtful and wonderfully clear writings of Daniel Migliore, to whom I am so very indebted for the substance that his writing has lent to my personal faith. Migliore deals brilliantly with religious pluralism in chapter 13 of his book *Faith Seeking Understanding,* and in this section I attempt to capture in short form what I consider the essentials of his ideas. To begin though, I think it will be helpful to address the definitional problem. My search for a simple and short definition of the word "pluralism" turned up several that I felt were at least partially lacking in clarity for our purposes here. But I found the following, more lengthy explanation of the term more useful:

> The plurality of religious traditions and cultures has come to characterize every part of the world today. But what is pluralism? Here are four points to begin our thinking:
> - First, pluralism is not diversity alone, but *the energetic engagement with diversity.* Diversity can and has meant the creation of religious ghettoes with little traffic between

---

[110] Migliore, *Faith Seeking Understanding,* 136, quoting Paul Helm, *The Providence of God* (Downers Grove: InterVarsity Press, 1994).

or among them. Today, religious diversity is a given, but pluralism is not a given; it is an achievement. Mere diversity without real encounter and relationship will yield increasing tensions in our societies.

- Second, pluralism is not just tolerance, but *the active seeking of understanding across lines of difference*. Tolerance is a necessary public virtue, but it does not require Christians and Muslims, Hindus, Jews, and ardent secularists to know anything about one another. Tolerance is too thin a foundation for a world of religious difference and proximity. It does nothing to remove our ignorance of one another, and leaves in place the stereotype, the half-truth, the fears that underlie old patterns of division and violence. In the world in which we live today, our ignorance of one another will be increasingly costly.

- Third, pluralism is not relativism, but *the encounter of commitments*. The new paradigm of pluralism does not require us to leave our identities and our commitments behind, for pluralism is the encounter of commitments. It means holding our deepest differences, even our religious differences, not in isolation, but in relationship to one another.

- Fourth, pluralism is *based on dialogue*. The language of pluralism is that of dialogue and encounter, give and take, criticism and self-criticism. Dialogue means both speaking and listening, and that process reveals both common understandings and real differences. Dialogue does not mean everyone at the "table" will agree with one another. Pluralism involves the commitment to being at the table—with one's commitments.[111]

Migliore begins his chapter on religious pluralism acknowledging the real and urgent need for Christian theology to engage in the development

---

[111] Diana Eck, "What is Pluralism?" The Pluralism Project at Harvard University. Available at http://www.pluralism.org/pages/pluralism/what_is_pluralism.

of "a theology of the religions" with "the distinctive theological task of asking about the place of the plurality of world religions...to clarify how it is possible to maintain the conviction that Jesus Christ is Lord and Savior of the world and at the same time to honor the integrity and value of other religions."[112] He deals interestingly with the "ambiguity of religion" from which he derives the conviction that a theology of religions today should be guided by two principles:

1. Recognition that there are real and not merely surface differences among world religions, and
2. While all religions of humanity command our respect, they are not beyond critical examination.[113]

Next Migliore discusses the typology of Christian theologies of the religions, describing a spectrum of positions ranging from "exclusivism," which asserts that Jesus Christ alone is the way, the truth and the life and there is no salvation other than through faith in Him, to "pluralism," which holds that all religions mediate knowledge of the mystery of God and all are equally valid ways of salvation.[114]

Migliore then builds on Paul Knitter's typology[115] (four types), introducing gradations of his own to arrive at a seven-type framework. He details each type carefully, and I recommend a full reading of his chapter 13 for a complete understanding of the progression of ideas along the spectrum of theologies considered. Here, though, for the sake of brevity I recite the essence of his points 3, 4 and 5, which I find the more interesting positions.

3. A third type teaches that Jesus Christ, the Savior and Lord of the world, is the "fullness" of God's truth and grace. All religions find their fulfillment in Christ. This view is represented by the *Document on the Relationship of the Church to Non-Christian Religions* (Nostra

---

[112] Migliore, *Faith Seeking Understanding*, 301.

[113] Migliore, *Faith Seeking Understanding*, 304–5.

[114] Migliore, *Faith Seeking Understanding*, 306.

[115] Paul Knitter, *Introducing Theologies of Religion* (Maryknoll: Orbis Books, 2002).

Aetate) adopted by the Vatican II Council.[116] According to the teaching of Vatican II, the non-Christian religions contain intrinsic values and possess authentic rays of truth about God. They can thus be seen as preparations for the reception of the fullness of the truth of the Christian gospel (*praeparatio evangelica*)...the grace of God in Jesus Christ does not destroy or replace truths found in other religions; it fulfills them.

4. Type 4...affirms that Jesus Christ alone is Savior and Lord of all, but it differs from them in holding that the saving grace of God decisively known in Jesus Christ is in some manner present to all people whether they have heard the Christian gospel or not. Salvation is therefore possible in and through other religions. This position...is most frequently associated with the theology of Karl Rahner, whose theology of the religions affirms the saving grace of Christ *within* the religions rather than seeing Christ as standing necessarily *against* the religions...Rahner's reasoning runs as follows. If, as Scripture teaches, God wills all persons to be saved (1 Tim. 2:4), and if God seeks to accomplish what God wills, the grace of God supremely manifest in Jesus Christ must be freely at work in all human life...Rahner not only holds that non-Christians can know some truths about God but also that they can come to a saving relationship with God if they respond faithfully to the knowledge that is made known to them, but also that other religions can be historical channels of a saving knowledge of God.

5. A fifth type primarily emphasizes the differences of the religions while being at the same time open to the possibility of salvation for those who have not heard of Jesus Christ or who in this life reject what they have heard. George Lindbeck,[117] a leading representative of this type...thinks that a theology of the religions like Rahner's neglects the real differences among the religions,

---

[116] William M. Abbott, ed., *The Documents of Vatican II* (New York: Guild Press, 1966), 660–71.

[117] See George Lindbeck, *The Nature of Doctrine: Religion and Theology in a Postliberal Age* (Philadelphia: Westminster, 1984).

trying unsuccessfully to build metaphysical (subtle, esoteric) bridges between the religions…for Lindbeck explicit confession and worship of Jesus Christ as Savior and Lord of all distinguishes Christian faith from the other religions…on the matter of the salvation of non-Christians, Lindbeck sees no reason why Christians may not hold that non-Christians encounter and receive the grace of Christ either in their last moments of life or in the life hereafter.[118]

Migliore draws Karl Barth into the discussion when he states that Barth argues that the capacity of Jesus Christ to address us

"is not restricted to his working on and in prophets and apostles and what is thus made possible and actual in his community." Jesus Christ speaks for himself in other witnesses than Bible and church…Barth also has distinctive reasons for remaining open to the possibility of universal salvation. He bases this possibility on the unequivocal Yes of God to humanity in Jesus Christ from the foundation of the world rather than on any speculation about what non-Christians might decide at death or after death…according to Barth, while Christians should not adopt a Universalist theology they have reason to hope and pray for the salvation of all.[119]

Finally, Migliore ties together these ideas about pluralism with our doctrine of God and the Trinity. Dupuis and Heim,[120] he says,

both believe that a Trinitarian understanding of God must be the centerpiece of a Christian theology of the religions… Dupuis contends that the Holy Spirit is active not only in the

---

[118] Migliore, *Faith Seeking Understanding*, 308–313 and 323.

[119] Migliore, *Faith Seeking Understanding*, quoting Karl Barth, *Church Dogmatics* 4 (Edinburgh: T. & T. Clark, 1978), 313 and 323.

[120] Jacques Dupuis, *Toward a Christian Theology of Religious Pluralism* (Maryknoll: Orbos Books, 1997) and Mark S. Heim, *The Depth of the Riches: A Trinitarian Theology of Religious Ends* (Grand Rapids: Eerdmans, 2001).

lives of individuals of other religious traditions but also in these religious traditions themselves. The Spirit of God is universally present and active…(but) Dupuis rejects any doctrine of God's saving grace that is centered on the Spirit separated from Christ…the work of Christ and the Spirit are two inseparable and complementary aspects of the one economy of salvation of the one triune God…and the Trinitarian reality of God is the basis of both the actuality and the theological legitimacy of religious pluralism.[121]

Heim contends that a Trinitarian inclusivism is the best alternative to exclusivism on the one hand and a relativistic pluralism on the other; "The Trinity is Christianity's pluralistic theology," Heim writes.[122]

The move toward a Trinitarian theology of the religions is consistent with the emphasis in this book (Migliore's, and mine) on the Trinitarian understanding of God revealed in Jesus Christ by the Holy Spirit and the understanding of salvation as the fulfillment of life in communion with God and other creatures.

We close out our discussion of religious pluralism with a recent statement approved by the 214th General Assembly of the Presbyterian Church (USA) that is carefully constructed to affirm both the uniqueness of the saving work of Jesus Christ and the freedom of God to accomplish God's purposes as God determines:

Jesus Christ is the only Savior and Lord, and all people everywhere are called to place their faith, hope and love in him. No one is saved by virtue of inherent goodness or admirable living, "for by grace you have been saved through faith, and this is not your own doing; it is the gift of God" (Eph. 2:8). No one is saved apart from God's gracious redemption in Jesus Christ. Yet we do not presume to limit the sovereign freedom of God our Savior, who desires everyone to be saved and to come to the knowledge of the truth (1 Tim. 2:3–4). Thus, we neither restrict the grace of God

---

[121] Taken from Migliore, *Faith Seeking Understanding*, 316–318.
[122] Heim, *The Depth of the Riches*, 33.

to those who profess explicit faith in Christ nor assume that all people are saved regardless of faith. Grace, love, and communion belong to God, and are not ours to determine.[123]

Barth's concern was "to let God be God" and to resist the temptation to imprison God in a conceptual system or a religious tradition.[124]

"Community" as God's Purpose

Migliore says,

> The doctrine of the church, or ecclesiology, is perhaps the least interesting and the most irritating topic of Christian theology. "Jesus yes, church no" nicely summarizes the anger and frustration that discussion of the church frequently arouses.[125]

I agree, but in recent years I have found a new way (new to me, that is) of seeing the church that has served to inject interest on my part, in the idea of more regular church attendance and participation more broadly in the activities and the initiatives of the church, and I would like to share this particular vision with you. The word that best describes the vision is "community," and what I am just coming to understand is that God's purpose importantly embraces a vision for community in which we can participate and share.

The interested reader will want to refer to part 5 of Stanley Grenz's book *Theology for the Community of God*, which deals extensively with the subject of ecclesiology.[126] Here my intent is simply to explain in a few paragraphs the essence of the concept of community in the Christian context as described by Grenz in other parts of his book. In the Christian context the idea of community extends from the concept of "the kingdom of God," which is

---

[123] *Hope in the Lord Jesus Christ*, Presbyterian Church USA General Assembly, 2002.

[124] Migliore, *Faith Seeking Understanding*, 316–323.

[125] Migliore, *Faith Seeking Understanding*, 248.

[126] Grenz, *Theology for the Community of God*, 461–570.

that order of perfect peace, righteousness, justice, and love that God gives to the world. This gift is (a "final days, divine purpose") concept for it comes in an ultimate way only at the renewal of the world consummated at Jesus' return. But the power of the kingdom is already at work, for it breaks into the present from the future. Therefore we can experience the kingdom in a partial yet vital manner en route to the great future day.[127]

Opposed to any movement in favour of community is Western culture's fascination with individualism, which centres on the "self-made and independent individual…independence rather than interdependence is our cultural bias."[128] However, Grenz states,

The modern Western fascination with individualism, however, is waning, especially within the human sciences. Many thinkers are realizing that our understanding of the human phenomenon must reflect a more adequate balance between its individual and social dimensions.[129]

This awareness has led to the development of a new model of the relationship between the individual and society called communalism, communitarianism or culturalism.[130]

The model insists,

Community is crucial to identity formation…community is crucial to the sustaining of character, virtue, and values. And it provides the necessary foundation for involvement in public discourse concerning matters of world view.[131]

---

[127] Grenz, *Theology for the Community of God*, 22.

[128] Migliore, *Faith Seeking Understanding*, 249.

[129] Daniel A. Helminiak, "Human Solidarity and Collective Union in Christ," *Anglican Theological Review* 70 (January 1988), 37.

[130] "Culturalism" is the term preferred by critic of the movement Robert J. McShea (*Morality and Human Nature: A New Route to Ethical Theory* [Philadelphia: Temple University Press, 1990], 89–148).

[131] Grenz, *Theology for the Community of God*, 23.

To this point,

Many human scientists have been exploring the thesis that our sense of personal identity develops through the telling of a personal narrative. Hence, finding ourselves means, among other things, finding the story in terms of which our lives make sense.[132]

Grenz comments,

The narrative of a person's life is always embedded in the story of the communities in which the person participates[133]...What purpose does the Creator seek to accomplish in and for the creation he is shaping?...The Father intends that creation share in his existence and enter into the relationship the Son enjoys with him. Thus, as the product of God's essence (which is love) and as God's counterpart, the world exists in order to participate in the life of the social Trinity.

We may summarize God's intention for the world by employing the term "community." Just as the triune God is the eternal fellowship of the Trinitarian members, so also God's purpose for creation is that the world participate in "community"...a redeemed people, living within a renewed creation, and enjoying the presence of their God...(this) idea is developed more fully in the closing chapters of the book of Revelation...(which) in addition to declaring the fullness of God's presence with his people, forms the climax of biblical anticipations of other dimensions of the ("final days, divine purpose") community God is seeking to bring to pass. The new order is pictured as a place in which nature will again fulfill its purpose of providing nourishment for all earthly inhabitants...and described in the ("final days, divine

---

[132] Robert N. Bellah, *Habits of the Heart: Individualism and Commitment in American Life*, Perennial Library edition (New York: Harper and Row, 1986), 81.
[133] See Alasdair MacIntyre, *After Virtue*, 2nd ed. (Notre Dame: University of Notre Dame Press, 1984), 221.

purpose") reality as a great and beautiful city, the new Jerusalem (Rev. 21:9–21). In that city, the peoples will live together in peace and harmony.

Consequently, the goal of community lies at the heart of God's actions in history. And God's ultimate intention for creation is the establishment of community.[134]

I conclude that church is our earthly opportunity to share in God's work towards the ultimate community; regardless of how imperfect our earthly church communities may be, churches are unique in their devotion to serve God and our world towards that order of perfect peace, righteousness, justice and love that God gives to the world. Can you conceive of a purpose more noble?

---

[134] Grenz, *Theology for the Community of God*, 51, 112-115.

CHAPTER 10

And That's a Wrap!

God Is God

Yeah, I believe in God, and God ain't me.
Even my money keeps telling me it's God I need to trust.
And I believe in God, but God ain't us.
Steve Earle

"Then you will know the truth, and the truth will set you free."
John 8:32

So there you have my story, my narrative, a "slice of life" embedded in the story of two communities—the institutional investment community and the community of Christian faith. The lessons I have learned from both communities are so intertwined as to be inseparable: lessons of governance, policy, risk management and faith and, within this framework, lessons about the importance of core values and leadership. And on leadership, lessons about humility and resolve.

Key takeaways? Whether investing our money or our lives we all need a clear statement of beliefs, a statement of faith as it were, to address things that are not seen and not knowable with certainty. You can't plan your investment strategy without a clear statement of investment beliefs, and you can't plan your life's strategy without a clear statement of faith. Our faith statement serves as a foundation, a springboard, for decisions and actions that ultimately determine who we are. Because our faith statement inescapably shapes our destiny, building our faith statement is inherently a very risky proposition. After all, we are dealing with things that are unseen and unknowable, and we could be wrong! But surely therein lies the excitement, the joy of life! Your beliefs will be right or they will be wrong, but they will free you to act with energy, focus and conviction in all that you do, reaping the joy that comes of the knowledge that you are fulfilling the purpose of your mandate, of your being, without reservation to the best of your ability. For "a man can do nothing better than to eat and drink and find satisfaction in his work" (Ecclesiastes 2:24).

So this is my faith—a theology that works for me and can work for you, a God who loves me and who loves you too. But if you don't agree with me, don't let that bother you—this is, after all, my faith, and my faith is just information observed, ideas shaped as I travel the road of my own personal spiritual journey. Of infinite importance to you is that you set your own destination, choose your route and embark on your journey, always growing and learning. Dig in, find the answers to your questions, reflect on them and shape your beliefs, your faith. Work it out "with fear and trembling" (Philippians 2:12), articulate it and live it…and embrace the risk that that entails. Therein, in the midst of your journey, in the search for truth, lies the joy of life!

I have enjoyed writing my story; I hope you have enjoyed reading it.

IMAGE REFERENCES

Frankfurt Stock Exchange
Taken from:
http://www.csmonitor.com/Business/The-Daily-Reckoning/2012/0515/The-financial-industry-s-growth-is-stunting-everything-else
(accessed August 3, 2013)

Wall Street Bull and Bear
Taken from:
http://www.freakingnews.com/Wall-Street-Bull-Pictures--2145-2.asp
(accessed August 3, 2013)

Trinity Church, Manhattan
Taken from:
http://www.ourtravelpics.com/photo/newyork_2/187/
(accessed August 19, 2013)

Ralph Cioffi Arrest
Taken from:
http://online.wsj.com/article/SB125530291552979141.html
(accessed August 3, 2013)

Wall Street Bull, Collapsed
Taken from:
http://www.avidtrader.com/2012/01/bulls-lose-steam-after-fed-high-wears-off/
(accessed August 3, 2013)

Portrait of Carl Friedrich Gauss
Taken from:
http://www.listsworld.com/greatest-mathematicians-of-all-time/
(accessed August 3, 2013)

Portrait of Jim Otar
Taken from:
http://www.youtube.com/watch?v=YrlVkAQJMKg
(accessed August 3, 2013)

Sixth Sense Movie Still
Taken from:
http://www.cinemaring.com/torrent/the-sixth-sense-1999-eng-dvdrip-hasak-torrent-f495119.html
(accessed August 3, 2013)

CASTLE QUAY BOOKS

www.ingramcontent.com/pod-product-compliance
Lightning Source LLC
Chambersburg PA
CBHW051727090426
42738CB00010B/2131